Golf Rules in Pictures

New and Revised Edition

Golf Rules in Pictures

Illustrated by George Kraynak
Revised and updated by Michael Brown

AN OFFICIAL PUBLICATION OF

The United States Golf Association®

A Perigee Book

A Perigee Book
Published by The Berkley Publishing Group
A division of Penguin Putnam Inc.
375 Hudson Street
New York, NY 10014

First edition: March 1993

The Penguin Putnam Inc. World Wide Web site address is
http://www.penguinputnam.com

Library of Congress Cataloging-in-Publication Data

United States Golf Association.
Golf rules in pictures / illustrated by George Kraynak ; revised and updated by Michael
Brown — New and rev. ed.
p.   cm.
"An official publication of The United States Golf Association."
Includes complete text of the Rules of Golf as approved
by The United States Golf Association and The Royal
and Ancient Golf Club of St. Andrews.
ISBN 0-399-51799-5 (alk. paper)
1. Golf—Rules. I. Kraynak, George. II. Brown, Michael.
III. Royal and Ancient Golf Club of St. Andrews. IV. Unites States Golf
Association. Rules of Golf. 1988. V. Title.
GV971.U5 1993   796.352'02'022—dc20   92-39631 CIP

Printed in the United States of America

11   12   13   14   15   16   17   18

CONTENTS

THE RULES OF GOLF   86

The complete text as approved by The United States Golf
Association and The Royal and Ancient Golf Club of St. Andrews, Scotland

INTRODUCTION

The Rules of Golf are not engraved in granite. In fact, like most rules and laws, they are subject to constant review and frequent interpretation.

The two governing bodies of the game—The United States Golf Association and The Royal and Ancient Golf Club of St. Andrews, Scotland—long ago recognized the need to have a unified set of Rules. There have been uniform Rules worldwide since 1952.

The USGA and the R&A write *The Rules of Golf* and have a combined "Decisions" service to interpret them. The Rules serve as the laws of our game, and the Decisions serve as legal precedents. While a knowledge of the Rules and Decisions may not help you play better golf, such knowledge can certainly enhance your enjoyment of the game and may even speed up your play.

I feel that I know the Rules quite well, but I still always carry a Rules book in my bag or pocket and have been a subscriber to the USGA's Decisions service for many years. In fact, several Rules situations that came up during tournaments involving me directly or indirectly have resulted in some of those Decisions being written or Rules being redefined.

I like to think, too, that my knowledge of the Rules—and a bit of reasonable stubbornness—played an important part in my first Masters victory. I was heading for that championship in 1958 as I played the par-three 12th hole in the final round. My tee shot flew the green and plugged in the soft ground between the putting surface and a bunker. The Rules official on the scene told me that I had no relief coming and must play the ball as it lay. I was not able to convince him that a Local Rule established for that round because of general wet conditions caused by a heavy overnight rain afforded me a free drop, so I informed him that I would play a second ball, taking a drop, and appealed his decision to the Committee. I took a five with the embedded ball, but a three with the second ball. My appeal was upheld, and I eventually won that Masters by a single stroke.

The average player may not have time to study the Rules book and learn every nuance of the 34 Rules it contains. After all, not everybody makes a living playing golf!

But it does make sense to know the Rules of the game. That's why I was pleased when I was asked to write an introduction to *Golf Rules in Pictures*, which has been designed and written to give the reader a working knowledge of the Rules.

The first Rules of Golf were written in Edinburgh, Scotland, more than 240 years ago. While there have been great changes in the game over the years, the three basic principles still apply: play the ball as it lies, play the course as you find it, and when it's not possible to do either, do what's fair.

This book should help you know how to do what's fair.

Arnold Palmer

ETIQUETTE

Be Considerate of Other Players

When one player is addressing the ball or making a stroke, you should not talk or stand too close to the ball or just behind the ball or the hole being played.

Don't Delay

For everyone's sake, don't delay the game and the play of others.

Safety First

Don't ever play until the players in front of you have moved out of range.

Playing Through During a Search For the Ball

If your party has stopped to search for a ball, signal to any players coming up from behind that they should pass. Make sure to wait until those players have passed before you go on with your own play.

Priority on the Course

If your party falls behind until there's more than one clear hole between your party and the players ahead, let the party behind you play through.

Holes in the Bunkers

If you make any holes or footprints in a bunker, smooth them away before you play on.

Replace Divots, Repair Ball-Marks and Damage by Spikes

Anytime you cut or displace any turf through the green, you should repair it immediately and carefully. If you damage the putting green, repair it as soon as your party completes the hole.

RIGHT   WRONG

Damage to the Greens

Try not to damage the putting green. Be careful about how you and your caddie put down your bag and place the flagstick. Don't stand too close to the hole, and when you remove the ball, do it carefully. Take care not to lean on your putter, especially as you lean over to retrieve the ball from the hole.

DEFINITIONS

Addressing the Ball

When you take a stance and ground your club, that's called "addressing the ball." Hazards are an exception, however; just taking a stance in a hazard is addressing the ball.

"Is my grip right?"

"Is the penalty one or two strokes?"

Advice

"Advice" in golf describes any suggestion given to a player that might affect how he or she plays, chooses a club, or makes a stroke.

It's okay to impart information about the Rules or about general information, such as where the hazards are or where flagsticks are placed on the putting green. This sort of information is not considered to be advice.

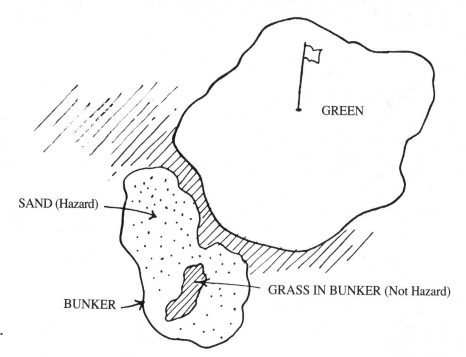

GREEN

SAND (Hazard)

GRASS IN BUNKER (Not Hazard)

BUNKER

Bunker

A bunker is a particular kind of hazard. It consists of an area, often a hollow or a depression, where the natural turf or soil has been replaced, usually with sand. The grass-covered ground around or inside a bunker is not part of the bunker. The bunker area extends down—no matter how far you dig toward China, you're still in the bunker; but it does not extend upward—the air, tree branches, etc., above the bunker are not part of the bunker.

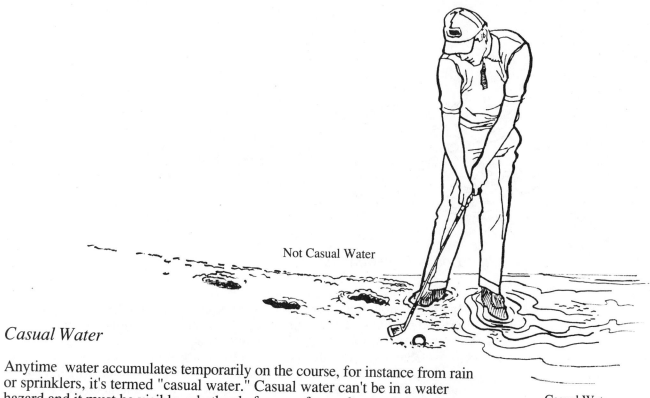

Not Casual Water

Casual Water

Casual Water

Anytime water accumulates temporarily on the course, for instance from rain or sprinklers, it's termed "casual water." Casual water can't be in a water hazard and it must be visible, whether before or after a player takes a stance. Snow and ice can be either casual water or loose impediments, whichever the player chooses; however, manufactured ice is an obstruction. Also, dew and frost are not casual water.

Ground Under Repair

"Ground under repair" is any part of the course that has been officially declared "under repair," and it may or may not be marked. The term includes heaped materials, holes made by the groundskeeper, and any items related to the repair and upkeep of the grounds. Ground under repair does not include groundkeeping debris that was intentionally abandoned and not meant to be marked or removed, such as grass or shrub cuttings.

If the area *is* marked, any stakes, lines, or signs *are* part of the ground under repair. As with bunkers, the boundary of the ground under repair extends down, but not up. Clubs are allowed to make Local Rules that prohibit playing from ground under repair.

Loose Impediments

The term "loose impediment" includes natural objects—twigs, leaves, branches, stones, animal droppings; insects, and any hills, homes, or husks created by them—that are not fixed, growing, or so solidly embedded that they can't be removed, and that do not become affixed to the ball.

Sand and soil are considered loose impediments only when they're on the putting green. The player decides in a given situation whether snow and ice are casual water or loose impediments, but manufactured ice is always an obstruction. Dew and frost are not loose impediments.

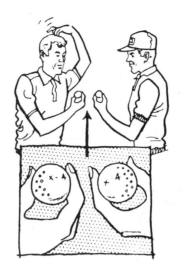

"I've found your first ball."
"I can't play that one—this one's in play now."

A Lost Ball

These conditions will determine that your ball is "lost":

- It can't be found or identified after you, your partner, or your caddies have searched for five minutes.
- You put another ball (a provisional ball) into play, whether or not there was a search for the first ball.
- You play any stroke with your provisional ball, whether from the likely location of the original ball or from a point nearer to the hole. At this point, the provisional ball becomes the ball in play.

Time spent playing a wrong ball doesn't count in the five-minute period of the search.

The Ball Moves

There are many instances in which various Rules will come into effect
because a ball moves. A ball is considered to have "moved" if it leaves its
position and comes to rest in any other place—an inch is as good as a mile.

Obstructions

An "obstruction" is anything artificial, including the surfaces and sides of
constructed paths and manufactured ice. Exceptions are:

- objects such as walls, fences, stakes, and railings that define out of
  bounds;
- any part of an immovable artificial object that's out of bounds;
- any construction that is considered to be an integral part of the
  course.

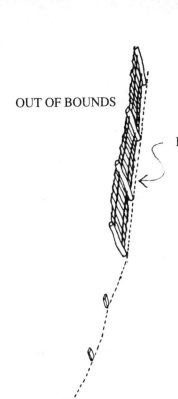

GOLF COURSE

WHITE LINE ON GROUND

OUT OF BOUNDS

OUT OF BOUNDS

Dotted line is out-of-bounds line

Out of Bounds

Any area where play is prohibited—the cemetery next to the course, for instance, or the walkway up to the clubhouse—is "out of bounds" for the ball. To be out of bounds, all of the ball has to lie completely beyond the boundary. The ball may touch the boundary and still be in bounds.

When a fence or stakes are used to define the out-of-bounds margin, the actual boundary line is determined by the nearest inside points of the stakes or fence posts at ground level. This holds true whether the stakes planted every few feet to show out of bounds are half an inch or four inches wide. If the ball completely crosses a line that a thread would draw between their inside corners, it's out of bounds.

Similarly, if out of bounds is marked by a line on the ground, the line itself is out of bounds. Although there's no physical object to mark it, the out-of-bounds line continues straight down through the ground and up to the sky.

As long as your ball is in bounds, you may step out of bounds to play it.

Outside Agency—Rub of the Green

An "outside agency" can be either a person or an object, but in match play it is not part of the match. For instance, your partner and everyone's golf bags are considered to be outside agencies. In the case of stroke play, the outside agency can be part of the game but not on the player's own side. Some examples of outside agencies include: a referee, a marker, a spectator, a forecaddie. Wind and water, however, are not outside agencies. When a ball in motion is accidentally deflected or stopped by an outside agency, this is a "rub of the green." Rule 19 covers how this situation is handled.

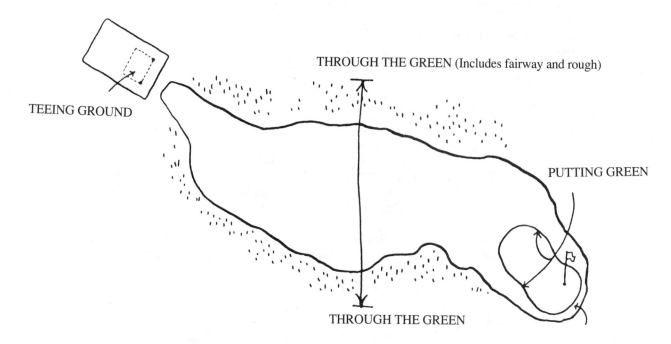

TEEING GROUND

THROUGH THE GREEN (Includes fairway and rough)

PUTTING GREEN

THROUGH THE GREEN

SHORT COLLAR OR APRON IS
NOT A PART OF PUTTING GREEN

Parts of the Course

Putting Green

The "putting green" is made up of all the ground surrounding the
hole that is especially prepared for putting, or has in some other way been
defined as the putting green.

Teeing Ground

The "teeing ground" is the area where the players begin to play a hole
or tee off. It should be rectangular, two club-lengths deep, and its front and
sides defined by two tee markers. A ball is considered to be outside the
teeing ground—similar to when it's out of bounds—if *all* of the ball is
outside the boundary.

Through the Green

The term "through the green" means the whole of the course, except:

•   the teeing ground and putting green of the hole being played, and
•   all the hazards.

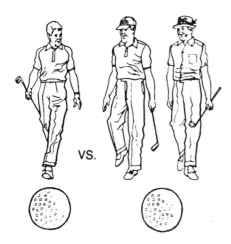

A **threesome** is a kind of match in which one player plays against two others. Each side plays one ball.

In a **foursome**, two players compete against two other players with each side playing one ball.

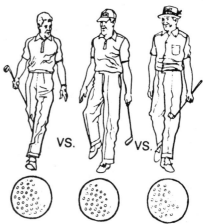

A **three-ball** match has three players, each competing against each of the others. Each has a ball and is playing two separate matches, one against each of the others.

A **best-ball** match may have three or four players. One player plays against the better ball of two or the *best* ball of three players.

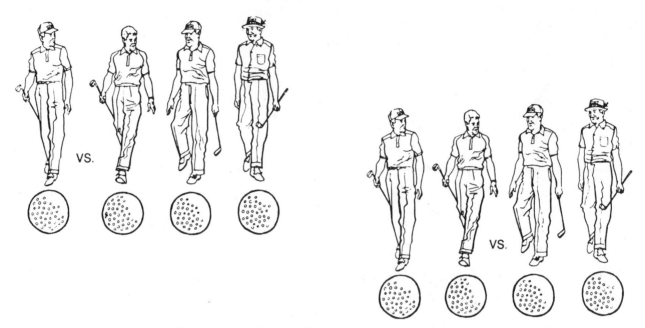

Finally, in a **four-ball** match two teammates each have a ball and play their better ball against the better ball of their two opponents.

Stroke

Anytime you move your club forward in an attempt to make a fair strike and to move the ball, you've taken a "stroke," even if you miss the ball. However, if you change your mind and check your stroke before the clubhead reaches the ball, it's not considered a stroke.

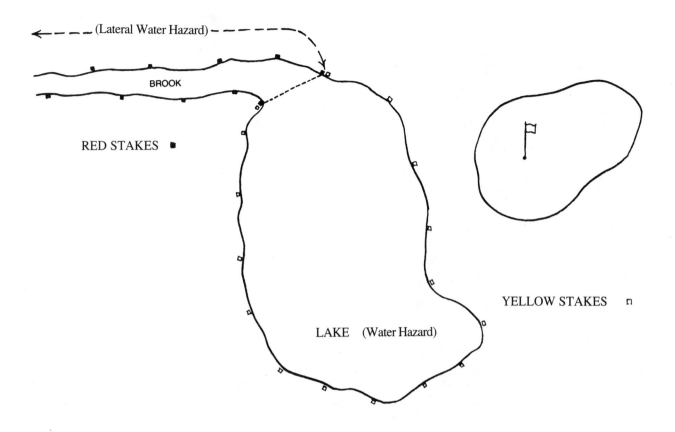

Water Hazards and Lateral Water Hazards

A "water hazard" is any sea, lake, pond, river, ditch, or similar body or course of water. Even if it's dried up, it's still a water hazard.

All the ground and all the water that lies within the margin of a water hazard is part of the hazard. Just as with bunker and ground-under-repair areas, the boundary of a water hazard extends upward and downward.

A "lateral water hazard" is any water hazard or part of one situated so that it's impossible to drop a ball behind the water hazard as described by Rule 26 and in the Definitions. When a water hazard or part of one is to be played as "lateral," it should be distinctively marked. The stakes and lines that define the margins of hazards are part of the hazards.

Water hazards should be defined by yellow stakes or lines, lateral water hazards by red stakes or lines.

Wrong Ball

A wrong ball is any ball other than:
- the ball in play;
- a provisional ball;
- a second ball played in stroke play under Rule 3–3 or Rule 20–7b.

THE RULES OF PLAY

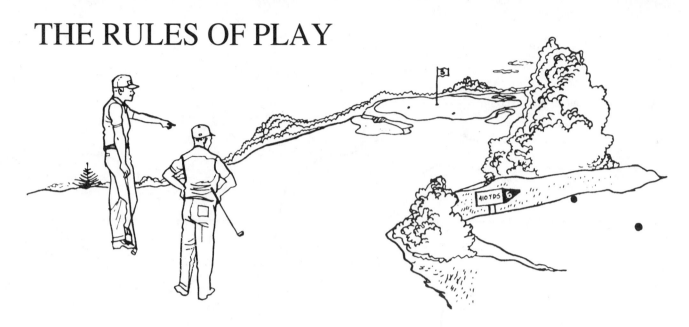

"We could save time by driving off the sixth tee before putting on the fifth."
"That would be wrong."

A Stipulated Round

In golf, the players play their balls from teeing grounds into holes by a succession of strokes—while following the rules, of course. **Rule 1–1.**

In a "stipulated round" the holes of the course are normally all played in the correct sequence—the first hole followed by the second, and so on. The Committee may specify otherwise.

A stipulated round has eighteen holes—but this, too, can be redefined by the Committee.

"Shall we play distance only for out of bounds?"

"No, indeed.

Agreeing to Waive the Rules

Players aren't allowed to agree among themselves to ignore any of the Rules or to ignore any penalties. Ignoring the Rules has penalties of its own: for match play, disqualification on both sides; in stroke play, disqualification of all the players involved. **Rule 1–3.**

Match Play

HOLE	1	2	3	4	5	6	7	8	9	OUT
FRANK	5	5	3	3	4	4	4			
BOBBY	4	4	2	3	4	4	4			

Holes Won   Holes Halved   Bobby winner of match 3 up and 2 to play.

Determining the Winner

Winner of a Hole; Reckoning of Holes

In match play, you win by winning holes; whoever wins the most holes wins the game. Except where the Rules say otherwise, a hole is won by the side who uses the fewest strokes to get the ball into the hole. In a handicap match, the match is won by the lowest net score.

The reckoning of holes is kept by the terms: so many "holes up" or "all square," and so many "to play."

A side is "dormie" when it is as many holes up as there are holes remaining to be played. **Rule 2–1.**

Mr. B is preparing to play his fourth stroke.
Mr. A, who has holed out in four, says to Mr. B, "Your putt is going to break to the left."

An Automatic Half

Halved Hole

A hole is halved if each side holes out in the same number of strokes. When a player has holed out and his opponent has been left with a stroke for the half, if the player thereafter incurs a penalty, the hole is halved. **Rule 2–2.**

Winner of a Match

Sometimes a point is reached in a match where one side can't win because the other side has already won more holes than are left to be played. In this case, the team that is ahead automatically wins.

Remember, a match will consist of a stipulated round, unless the ruling Committee says otherwise. In case of a tie, the Committee may add holes to the round until the tie is broken. **Rule 2–3.**

Concession of the Next Stroke, Hole, or Match

When your ball is literally teetering on the edge of the hole but doesn't fall in, your opponent may concede that it inevitably would be put in on the next stroke. Then you don't have to actually tap the ball in with your putter—just score the stroke, pick up your ball, and continue the round. However, your ball must be "at rest" as described by Rule 16–2.

Any player is allowed to concede a hole or a match at any time before the hole or match is finished. Once someone concedes, the opponent can't force him to play it out, and the one who concedes may not change his mind, either. **Rule 2–4.**

"Did you break a Rule on the last hole when you dropped away from that fence?"

Claims in Match Play

Claims

If any dispute arises among players during a match and no one of authority is available to quickly resolve the matter, go on with the match. Once any player in the match tees from the next teeing ground, or after the last hole when all the players have left the putting green, the Committee can't consider any claims.

A Committee will consider a later claim only if the player making the claim bases it on facts previously unknown and if an opponent gave wrong information to the player. Further, the Committee won't consider *any* claim after the result of the match has been officially announced, unless the opponent gave the wrong information *deliberately*. **Rules 6–2a, 9, and 2–5.**

Penalty

Unless otherwise provided, the penalty in match play for a breach of the Rules is that you lose a hole. That is the penalty for breaking the Rules we describe from this point on, unless otherwise stated. **Rule 2–6.**

Stroke Play

Determining the Winner

In stroke play, you win by completing the round with fewer strokes than any of the other players. **Rule 3–1.**

HOLE	OUT	10	11	12	13	14	15	16	17	18	IN	TOTAL
FRANK	38	5	3	3	4	5	4	3	4	5	36	74
BOBBY	35	5	4	4	4	5	5	3	4	3	37	72

Bobby is the winner.

"This is a gimme."
"No! This is stroke play. You must hole out."

Failure to Hole Out

In stroke play, you must hole out—your ball must enter each and every hole on every putting green. If even once you fail to hole out before you take a stroke on the next hole (or, on the last hole, before you leave the putting green), you'll be disqualified. **Rule 3–2.**

Doubts About Procedure

Procedure

If during stroke play on a hole you get confused about what you're allowed or supposed to do in a certain situation, you're allowed to play a second ball. Before doing anything, however, you *must* tell the other players what you're up to and which ball you'll score with.

Unless both your balls scored the same, you must tell the Committee about what happened before turning in your score card. If you don't do this, you will be disqualified.

Determination of Score for a Hole

If what you decided to do *after* you were confused turned out to be the legal course to take, then that second ball will be your score.

But, if you don't announce your decision in advance and say that you are operating under Rule 3–3, your first ball in play—if legal—will count for the score. **Rule 3–3.**

"There's no penalty given for breaking that Local Rule."

"I think this should be ground under repair.

I'll play this ball as it lies, and a second ball

under Rule 3–3. I want to score with the second ball."

Penalty

The penalty in stroke play for a breach of the Rules is the addition of two strokes to your score. This is the penalty for breaking the Rules described, unless otherwise specified. **Rule 3–5.**

The Equipment

The Club

Moveable Parts Prohibited

You have some leeway about what kind of equipment you may take out on the course, but there are also some Rules you must follow. A club, for instance, must have a head and a shaft that are one unit and not detachable from each other. Except for weight, the club can't be adjustable and it can't, in general, veer too drastically away from the traditional design of a golf club. **Rule 4–1a.**

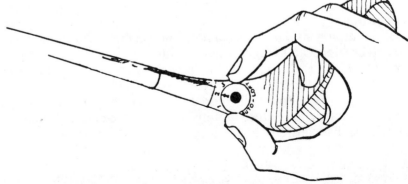

CLUB GRIP (Circular)

PUTTER GRIP (Flat Side—Permitted on Putters Only)

The Grip

The do's and don'ts of clubs are spelled out in the Rules. In particular, be careful about the restrictions on the grip—the part of the shaft that you hold onto—and any material added to it. It must be more or less straight, plain, and round, with no finger molds or the like. The exception is the putter, whose grip can be noncircular as long as it's not concave. **Rule 4–1c, Appendix II.**

"Let's be sure I have only fourteen clubs."

A Maximum of Fourteen Clubs

Selecting, Replacing, and Sharing Clubs

You may not start a round with more than fourteen clubs. Once you've selected your fourteen clubs, you must use those and not switch them for others. You may, however, start with fewer than fourteen, then add some later—which then become a permanent part of the set for that round. If a club becomes broken or unfit for play, you may replace it, but you're not permitted to borrow a club that someone else is using.

You may share clubs with your partner, but you still must not have more than fourteen clubs between you.

If you break these Rules in match play, you're going to lose one hole for each hole where you were in error, but not more than two holes on a given round. In stroke play, you'll lose two strokes for each hole where the breach occurred, with a maximum loss per round of four strokes. **Rules 4–4a,b.**

Excess Club Declared Out of Play

Once you discover that you're carrying too many clubs, you must immediately announce that you're taking the extra club(s) out of play, and don't use it again. If you fail to do this, you can be disqualified. **Rule 4–4c.**

The Ball

Balls can't weight more than 1.62 ounces and can't be smaller than 1.68 inches in diameter. If you use a ball that doesn't comply with these specs, you'll be disqualified.

Also, you're not allowed to put materials on your ball to improve its performance.

"Isn't that a small ball you're using?"

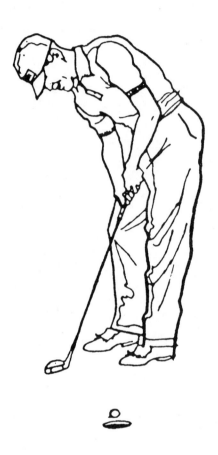

"Yes—but I use it only once in a while."

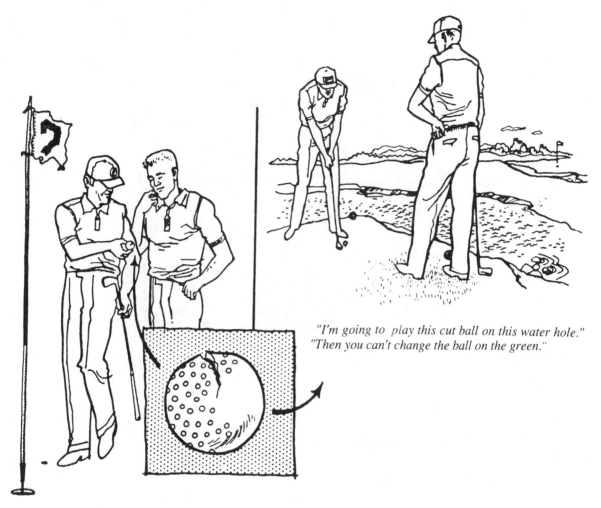

"I'm going to play this cut ball on this water hole."
"Then you can't change the ball on the green."

Ball Unfit For Play

A ball that doesn't look good—one that's scratched, muddy, or has its paint scraped—is still fit to use. However, if it is cut, cracked, or misshapen, it's "unfit for play" and you should not use it. Tell the other players what you're doing before you pick it up to replace it, and let a competitor see the condition of the ball and concur that it *is* unfit. You're not allowed to clean the ball up to prove it's unfit (Rule 21). If someone disputes the ball's fitness, they must do it before you place the new ball. When you place a new ball, be sure to put it just where the old one was.

If a ball falls to pieces as you stroke it, you're allowed to take the stroke again with a new ball, with no penalty. **Rule 5–1,2,3.**

Player's Responsibilities

Conditions of Competition

It's up to you to know the Rules and to find out about and know any special conditions of a given competition. **Rule 6–1.**

Checking Handicaps

Match Play

It's up to you and the other players to find out each other's handicaps before starting a handicap competition.

If it is discovered that a player has declared a too-high handicap—one that affects the number of strokes given or received—and begins a handicap match, the player will be disqualified. If the inaccuracy of the handicap is not high enough to affect the strokes, the player may go ahead and play that handicap. **Rule 6–2a.**

Stroke Play

You must make sure, anytime you play a handicap round, that your handicap is recorded on your card before you turn it over to the Committee. If it's not there or is too high—to the point that it affects the number of strokes—you can be disqualified. It's also up to you to know at which holes handicap strokes are given. **Rule 6–2b.**

Breach of a Rule by a Caddie

Each player is allowed only one caddie—the penalty is disqualification.
When your caddie breaks a Rule, you, the player, take the proper penalty.
Rule 6–4.

"Those last fellows certainly scuffed up the green."

"You can't do that."

Identifying Your Ball

It's up to you, once play is under way, to make sure you go on playing the same ball. Mark your ball so you'll know it's yours. **Rule 6–5.**

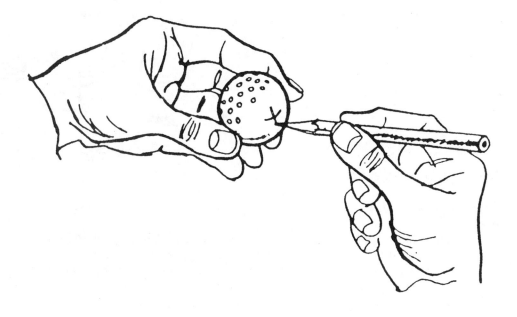

Signing and Returning Your Card

At the end of the round each player is responsible for making sure his or her score for each hole has been recorded correctly. If you have a point of doubt in your mind, take it up with the Committee at once. Sign the card, make sure the marker has signed it too, and get it to the Committee promptly at the end of the round. Failing to do any of this can get you disqualified. **Rule 6–6b.**

"May I see that card I turned in about an hour ago? I think I put down a five for the eighteenth hole, but I actually had a six."

Scoring in Stroke Play

Once the scorecards have been turned in, no changes may be made. **Rule 6–6c.**

The final responsibility rests with you for making sure your score is correctly recorded for each hole. If you record a higher score than you should have, it's going to stand; but if the score is lower than it should have been, you'll be disqualified. **Rule 6–6d.**

You don't add the scores yourself; the Committee does that, and they also take care of applying the handicap to your final score.

For four-ball stroke play there are further restrictions. See Rule 31–4 and 31–7a.

Undue Delay

When you finish a hole, get on with the next one! The Rules say you must not cause "undue delay" between the end of one hole and the tee-off of the next. The standard penalties apply (in match play, a hole; in stroke play, two strokes), and if you keep on causing this kind of delay, you can be disqualified. **Rule 6–7.**

Discontinuing Play

As much as you might hate it when you are playing well, sometimes a round of golf must be stopped. You are allowed to—and sometimes you *must*—stop playing if:

• the Committee suspends play;
• you believe there's danger from lightning;
• there's some doubt or dispute and you're waiting on a decision from the Committee (take a look also at Rules 2–5 and 34–3); or
• another *good* reason exists, such as sudden illness.

Unpleasant weather is not enough reason to stop playing, but sometimes you must stop play for some reason without permission from the Committee—for instance, sudden thunder and lightning. In this case, report to the Committee as soon as you can. If they agree that your reason was good, there's no penalty. If they don't buy it, you'll be disqualified. **Rule 6–8a.**

There's an exception for match play: All the players in a match can agree to discontinue without penalty, unless you cause a larger competition to be delayed.

To momentarily leave the course does not necessarily mean you have discontinued play.

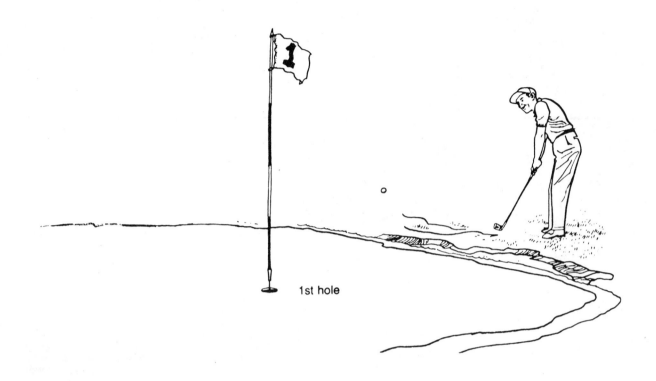

1st hole

Practice

Golf takes a lot of practice, but you're not supposed to be practicing *while* you're playing. Numerous Rules govern when *you may not* practice.

Before or Between Rounds

Match Play

On any day of a match play competition, players are allowed to practice on the course before the competition begins. **Rule 7–1a.**

Stroke Play

On any day of a stroke competition or play-off, you may *not* practice on the competition course. You also may not test the surface of any of the putting greens on the course. When rounds of a stroke competition are being played on consecutive days, you're not allowed to practice on the course between rounds.

The only kind of practice allowed is practice putting or chipping on or near the teeing ground before you start a round or play-off.

If you practice when you shouldn't, the penalty is disqualification. **Rule 7–1b.**

During Play of Hole

"Watch out, Hank; I'm playing another shot for practice."

Between Holes

"Can't do it—it's against the Rules."

"As long as we have to wait, don't you think it would be all right if we tried a few practice putts on the ninth green?"

During Round

During a round of golf, you may not practice strokes while you're playing a hole or between two holes. You are allowed to practice putting or chipping on or near the putting green that was last played, on any practice putting green, or on the teeing ground of the next hole you'll be playing. Also, you may not practice strokes from a hazard, even between holes. And remember, even the practice that is allowed can't be done if it delays play.

Also note that a practice *swing* is not a practice *stroke*. You can practice your swing anywhere, as long as you don't violate any other Rules by doing so. **Rule 7–2.**

Advice; Indicating the Line of Play

Giving or Asking For Advice

As mentioned in the Definitions section, advice in golf concerns suggestions about how to play, choose a club, or make a stroke. You're allowed to give this kind of advice only to your partner, and you may take it only from your partner, your caddie, and your partner's caddie. **Rule 8–1.**

"Fine shot. What club did you use?"

"Your line is straight over the bag."
"That's against the Rules. Take the bag away, please."

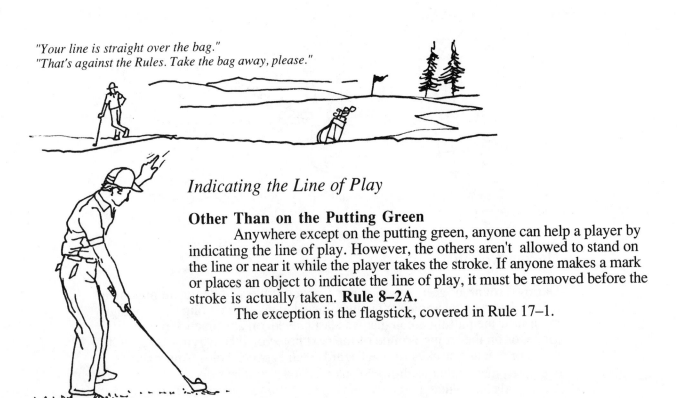

Indicating the Line of Play

Other Than on the Putting Green

Anywhere except on the putting green, anyone can help a player by indicating the line of play. However, the others aren't allowed to stand on the line or near it while the player takes the stroke. If anyone makes a mark or places an object to indicate the line of play, it must be removed before the stroke is actually taken. **Rule 8–2A.**

The exception is the flagstick, covered in Rule 17–1.

On the Putting Green

Special restrictions dictate how players may indicate the line of play on the putting green. When your ball is on the green, your partner or either of the caddies may point out the putting line, but only before your stroke, not during it, and they must not touch the green or mark it. **Rule 8–2b.**

"Putt it for here."

Club touching green

WRONG

Club held off green

RIGHT

"I lie five, and not four as I said before you played your last shot. I forgot to include a penalty on my second shot. Sorry."

Information About the Number of Strokes Taken

General

The number of strokes a player has taken includes any penalty strokes up to that point. **Rule 9–1.**

Match Play

When you are penalized, you must promptly inform your opponent—unless it is obvious that your opponent has observed enough to know you have been penalized. If you don't tell an opponent the penalty, you are giving wrong information. This is true even if you yourself weren't aware of the penalty.

During the play of a hole, opponents are allowed to ask and if asked must give the number of strokes they've taken so far. If asked, they also must tell how many strokes they've taken for a hole that was just completed.

If you give wrong information to an opponent about the number of strokes you've taken, it's important to correct the error before your opponent takes the next stroke. If you don't correct it before that stroke, you'll lose the hole.

If the hole is finished and you give wrong information that might affect your opponent's understanding of the hole's result, correct your error before anyone tees off from the next hole. If you do, there's no penalty. If someone tees off (or on the last hole, if everyone leaves the putting green) and you haven't corrected the error, you lose the hole. **Rule 9–2.**

Order of Play

On the Teeing Ground and Elsewhere

On the first tee, the players draw lots to see who goes first.

Match Play

In match play, whoever wins a hole plays first on the next hole; that's called having the "honor." When the balls are in play elsewhere than on the teeing ground, the ball farthest from the hole is played first. If the balls are the same distance from the hole, draw lots to see who plays first. **Rule 10–1a,b.**

Stroke Play

In stroke play, the low scorer takes the honor on a new hole, the next lowest scorer goes next, and so on. If two or more competitors have the same score for a hole, they tee off in the same order as they did on the previous hole. **Rules 10–2a,b.**

"I believe it was my honor."

Playing out of Turn

Match Play

If you play at your opponent's turn, there's no penalty; however, your opponent can make you cancel the stroke and take it again in the right order, placing the ball exactly where it had been. **Rule 10–1c, Rule 20–5.**

Stroke Play

There's no penalty for playing out of turn in stroke play; the ball is played as it lies. However, if competitors agree to play in an order differing from the one described above for the purpose of giving someone an advantage, they'll all be disqualified. **Rule 10–2c.**

Out of Bounds

Who drives next?

Second Ball From the Teeing Ground

If you play a provisional or second ball from the teeing ground, you must wait until your opponent or fellow-competitor has played his first stroke. If you don't wait, you're out of turn: in match play you may have to replay the stroke from the spot, and in stroke play (Rule 10–2c) you could be disqualified. **Rule 10–3.**

Teeing Ground

Ball Falling off the Tee

If your ball falls off the tee before it's in play—or if you knock it off as you address it—you may replace it on the tee. However, if you take a stroke at it in this situation, your stroke counts. There's no penalty in either case.

Stance legal

Ball's position wrong

Playing Outside the Teeing Ground

You are supposed to start the hole by playing a ball from inside the teeing ground. If you play from outside the area, you will suffer these consequences:

Match Play
Your opponent can make you cancel the stroke and play again from within the area.

Stroke Play
You're penalized two strokes and must take the stroke again from within the area. If you reach the next teeing ground and make a stroke without having replayed the previous stroke—or on the last hole, leave the putting green without stating your intention to correct it—you'll be disqualified. Any strokes taken from outside the teeing ground won't count in your score. **Rule 11–4b.**

Teeing; Tee-Markers
You may stand outside the teeing ground to play a ball that's inside the teeing ground. **Rule 11–1.**
Once the tees are fixed, however, you aren't allowed to fool around with them to help your stance. **Rules 11–2 and 13–2.**

Searching For the Ball; Identifying the Ball

Searching For and Seeing the Ball

It's okay, when you're looking for your ball, to handle long grass, bushes, and so forth—but only for the purpose of searching, and not to enhance the lie of the ball, the area of your swing, or your line of play. **Rule 12–1.**

If your ball lands in a hazard and becomes covered by loose impediments or sand, you may remove the covering so you can see part of the ball. If you remove too much and completely uncover the ball, you aren't penalized as long as you re-cover the ball until it's only partly visible. If you accidentally move the ball, replace it and re-cover it. Rule 23 explains how you may remove loose impediments outside a hazard.

If, while searching for your ball, you accidentally move it from casual water, an area of ground under repair, a hole, or an animal burrow, again, you may replace it without penalty. Unless, that is, you decide to seek "relief," as described in Rule 25–1b.

If you don't see your ball and you think it's submerged in a water hazard, you may fish for it with your club or your hands. However, if you find it, you must leave it where it was; if you move it, you must put it back. If you take care to do that, there's no penalty—unless you choose an option in Rule 26–1.

"My ball must be buried in the sand."

Are you always allowed to see the ball when you play?

"I'm sure the ball is here someplace."

May he lift the ball?

Yes   No   Sand in bunker

Identifying the Ball

Anywhere but in a hazard you're allowed to lift a ball to make sure it's yours; and to clean it enough so that it can be identified. Before you lift it, however, tell your opponents or fellow-competitors so they can watch you do it. If you don't give them this opportunity, it can cost you a stroke. If it *is* your ball, replace it where it was and take your stroke. **Rule 12–2.**

Playing the Ball as It Lies;
Area of Intended Swing and Line of Play;
Stance

Playing the Ball as It Lies

Many provisions in the Rules concern balls that have difficult lies. Unless a particular situation is addressed in one of these Rules, the ball must be played as it lies. **Rule 13–1.**

For what to do about a ball at rest that moves, see Rule 18.

Improving the Lie, Area of Intended Swing, or Line of Play

Unless it's allowed somewhere else in the Rules, you are not allowed to improve:

- the position or lie of your ball;
- the area where you will be swinging;
- your line of play;
- the extension of that line beyond the ball; or
- the area where you're going to drop or place the ball.

"Do you want me to hold back this limb?"

How hard may a player press down the grass?

Specifically, you are prohibited from making those improvements via any of these actions:

- moving, bending, or breaking anything that is growing or fixed, including any immovable obstructions or any object that marks the out-of-bounds limits; or
- removing or pressing down sand, loose soil, replaced divots, any cut turf placed in position, or any other surface irregularity.

It's okay in some instances to do some of that moving, breaking, pressing, etc., but only if:

- it occurs while you're normally taking your stance;
- it happens as you're making your stroke, or as you move the club back to take the stroke;
- it's part of creating or eliminating surface irregularities on the teeing ground; or
- it takes place on the putting green as you remove sand and loose soil (which is covered in Rule 16–1a and 16–1c).

With the above exceptions, take care that when you ground your club, you only do so lightly and don't press it down. **Rule 13–2.**

This is wrong

Building a Stance

The Rules are designed to stop you from improving the lie of the ball, your swing area, etc., but you are allowed to place your feet firmly as you take a stance. Take care, however, not to build it—that is, to stand on something, create a mound to stand on, and so forth. **Rule 13–3.**

Ball Lying in or Touching a Hazard

The situation differs regarding hazard balls. Unless it's covered elsewhere in the Rules, before you take a stroke at a ball in or touching a bunker or a water hazard, you're not allowed to:

- test the condition of the hazard or one like it;
- touch the ground or the water in the hazard with your hands or clubs or anything else;
- handle any loose impediment in or touching the hazard.

There are some exceptions:

- It's okay to touch the ground or water in a hazard because you fall or nearly fall while legally removing an obstruction, measuring, or retrieving or lifting a ball—but you must not do anything to deliberately test the hazard or improve the lie of your ball.

- After your stroke, you may smooth the sand or soil in the hazard, and your caddie may do so anytime, without your authority. However, if the ball is still in the hazard, neither of you may do anything to improve the lie of your ball or to help you as you continue to play the hole.

Lest you are now afraid to move or touch anything, remember: During your address and as you swing the club back, it's okay if your club *touches* any obstruction, construction, or integral part of the course, as well as any grass, bush, tree, or any other growing thing. **Rule 13–4.**

Water

Bunker

Loose impediments must not be touched

Smoothing Irregularities

Striking the Ball

Wrong

Striking the Ball Fairly; Assistance

You must strike fairly at the ball, and not use your club to scrape, hook, or spoon the ball. **Rule 14–1.**

While making your stroke, you're not allowed to have physical assistance or protection from the elements. **Rule 14–2.**

Artificial Devices and Unusual Equipment

You are not allowed to use artificial devices or unusual equipment to gauge or measure distance or conditions that affect you play. You're also not allowed to use any such devices to help you grip the club, make a stroke, or assist you in your play. If you do, you can be disqualified. **Rule 14–3.**

Plain gloves are allowed, and you may put resin, tape, gauze, or a towel or other cloth on the grip of the club (within the parameters of **Rule 4–1c**).

Striking the Ball More Than Once

If you hit the ball more than once during a stroke, you'll have to add a penalty, making a total of two strokes. **Rule 14–4.**

Playing a Moving Ball

In general, you're not permitted to play your ball while it's moving. Various exceptions and special conditions are:

- when the ball falls off the tee (Rule 11–3);
- when you strike the ball more than once (Rule 14–4);
- a ball moving in water (Rule 14–6).

   If the ball moves after you begin your stroke or during the back motion for the stroke, there's no penalty. However, you still must follow the other Rules regarding moving the ball (18–2a), the ball moving after address (18–2b), and the ball moving after a loose impediment is touched (18–2c). **Rule 14–5.**

Ball Moving in Water
   There's no penalty for taking a stroke at a ball that's moving in a water hazard. You are not, however, allowed to wait and watch in hopes of the wind or current putting your ball in a better position for you. Under Rule 26, you may lift the ball.

Playing a moving ball is prohibited . . . but . . .

a water hazard is different.

Playing a Wrong Ball

A "wrong" ball is any ball that isn't in play, a provisional ball, or (in stroke play) a second ball played under Rule 3–3 or 20–7b.

"Ball in play," by the way, includes a ball substituted for the one in play in cases where substitution is permitted.

General

Unless you make a legal substitution, you must play the ball you started with all the way into the hole. If you make an illegal substitution, you'll be penalized. Strokes with the wrong ball in a hazard are not penalized, so long as you then go ahead and play the correct ball. Strokes with the wrong ball don't count in a player's score. **Rule 15–2,3.**

Match Play

If you make a stroke with a wrong ball anywhere but in a hazard, you lose the hole. When you and your opponent exchange balls during a hole, the first to play the wrong ball loses the hole. If you really can't figure out who did what and when the balls were exchanged, then go ahead and play the hole out with the balls exchanged. **Rule 15–2.**

Stroke Play

For a stroke with a wrong ball, you get a two-stroke penalty. After being penalized, finish play with the correct ball, unless you've made a stroke on the next teeing ground or, on the last hole, have left the putting green. **Rule 15–3.**

The Putting Green

Touching the Line of Putt

Don't touch the line of putt! Having said that, here is what you *may* do:

- On the putting green, you may move sand, loose soil, and other loose impediments. Pick them up or brush them aside with your hand or club without pressing down.
- When addressing the ball, it's okay to place the club in front of the ball, just don't press anything down.
- You may touch the line of putt while measuring (Rule 10–4), lifting the ball, pressing down a ball marker, repairing old hole plugs or ball marks on the putting green, or removing movable obstructions (Rule 24–1). **Rule 16–1a,b,c.**

For more information on indicating the line for putting on putting green, see Rule 8–2b.

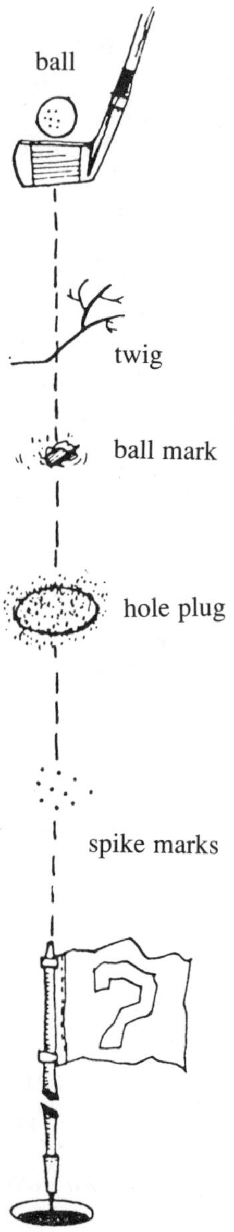

ball

Club may be placed in front of ball without pressing anything down

Loose impediment may be removed

twig

ball mark

May be repaired

hole plug

May not be repaired

spike marks

Standing Astride or on the Line of Putt

Don't make a stroke on the putting green while straddling the line of putt, or with either foot touching the line or the line's extension beyond the ball. **Rule 16–1e.**

Position of Caddie or Partner

While making a stroke, don't let your caddie, your partner, or your partner's caddie get on or close to an extension of the line of putt behind the ball. **Rule 16–1f.**

Playing a Stroke While Another Ball Is in Motion

Don't play a stroke while another ball is in motion after a stroke on the putting green. However, there won't be a penalty if it was your turn to play. **Rule 16–1g.**

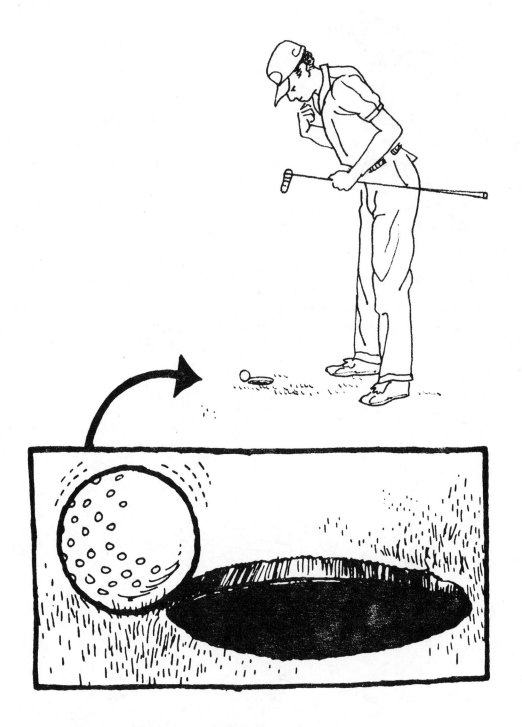

Ball Overhanging the Hole

Oh so close! If your ball is hanging over the edge of the hole, the Rules allow you time to get there and then ten more seconds to wait and see if it will roll in. If it doesn't fall in until after ten seconds, add a stroke to your score. Regarding other kinds of undue delay, see Rule 6–7. **Rule 16–2.**

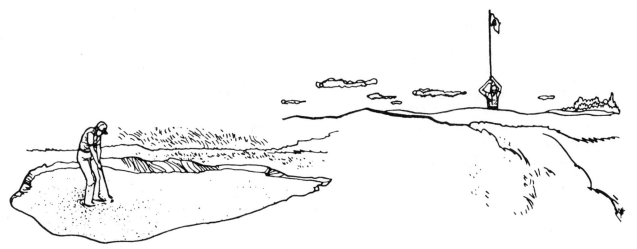

The Flagstick

Attended, Removed, or Held Up

Right before and while you're making your stroke, you may have someone take up the flagstick and use it to indicate the position of the hole. But remember, they can do it only at your request. If you see someone using the flagstick to position the hole for you and you don't object, you have de facto authorized it. Anyone holding the flagstick or standing near the hole during your stroke is officially attending the flagstick until the ball comes to rest. **Rule 17–1.**

Unauthorized Attendance

In match play, when you're making a stroke or your ball is in motion, the opposing player and caddie aren't allowed to attend, remove, or hold up the flagstick without your authorization, and will be penalized for doing so.

In stroke play, fellow-competitors and caddies aren't allowed to handle the flagstick without your authority, and will be penalized for doing so. If your ball strikes the flagstick while they're holding it, there's no penalty and you'll play the ball as it lies, unless the stroke was played from the putting green. In that case, the stroke is canceled. Place the ball back where it was before the stroke and make the stroke again.

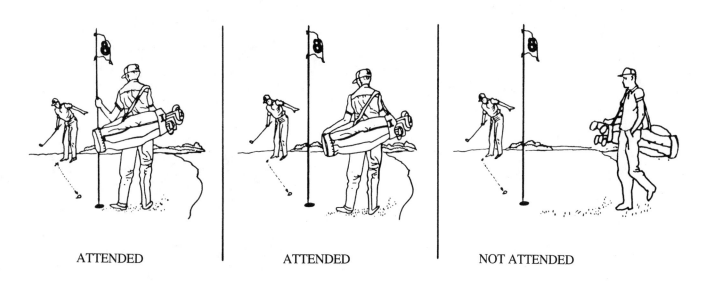

ATTENDED   ATTENDED   NOT ATTENDED

Ball Striking Flagstick or Attendant

You're not allowed to hit these things with your ball:

- the flagstick when you're handling it or anyone else is handling it with your knowledge and authority;
- any person holding the flagstick with your authority or prior knowledge, or anything being carried by that person;
- the flagstick in the hole, unattended, when the ball has been played from the putting green.

Rule 17–3.

Flagstick Unattended; Play from the Green

Flagstick Unattended; Play off Green

Flagstick Attended; Play from or off Green

When the Ball Rests Against the Flagstick

If the ball comes to rest against the flagstick in the hole, you're allowed to remove the flagstick from the hole, or have someone else do it for you. If the ball falls in, then you've holed out. If the ball moves, but doesn't go in, put it back where it was and you'll have to use another stroke to get it in. **Rule 17-4.**

Ball Moved or Deflected

By an Outside Agency

You won't be penalized if a ball at rest is moved by an outside agency, as explained in Definitions. Replace the ball before playing another stroke. Rule 18–5 will explain what to do when your ball is moved by another ball. **Rule 18–1.**

"Drop that ball."

By Player, Partner, Caddie, or Equipment

General

Except where the Rules allow, you may not purposely touch, lift, move, or cause your ball to move when it's in play—except, of course, with your club as you address the ball. Your partner and your caddies aren't allowed to either, and doing so will cost you a penalty stroke. There's also a penalty stroke if your or your partner's equipment causes the ball to move.

After the illegal move, replace the ball where it was, unless you had already begun your swing when the ball moved and did not stop.

There is no penalty if you accidentally cause your ball to move while:

- measuring to see which ball is farther from the hole (Rule 10–4);
- searching for a covered ball in a hazard or one in casual water or in ground under repair (Rule 12–1);

"You shouldn't have lifted my ball out of the divot."

Caddie A

A's ball

"Gosh, Mr. A—I moved your ball. That's a penalty."

- repairing a hole plug or ball mark (Rule 16–1c) or removing a loose impediment on the putting green (Rule 18–2c);
- lifting a ball (Rule 20–1) or placing or replacing it (Rule 20–3a);
- complying with the Rule regarding lifting the ball, interfering with, or assisting play (Rule 22);
- removing a movable obstruction (Rule 24–1).

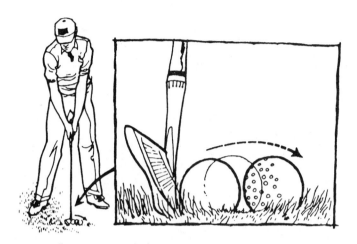

Ball Moving After Address

If you move your ball as you address it, you'll get a penalty stroke and have to replace the balls. However, if the ball moves after you begin your stroke and you don't stop the stroke, there's no penalty, but the stroke counts. **Rule 18–2b.**

Ball Moved by Opponent, Caddie, or Equipment —In Match Play

During a Search
If an opponent moves your ball, or the opponent's caddie or equipment moves it, while helping to search for it, there's no penalty and you must replace the ball. **Rule 18–3a.**

Player B

Player A

B's ball

"Sorry, Mr. B—I guess I kicked your ball."

Not During a Search

However, if an opponent or the opponent's caddie or equipment moves your ball and they're not searching for it, your opponent is penalized one stroke. Some exceptions are described in Rules 10–4, 18–2, and 22.

After your opponent is penalized, replace the ball. **Rule 18–3b.**

Ball Moved by a Fellow-Competitor, Caddie, or Equipment— In Stroke Play

During a Search, or Not

If a player's ball is moved by a fellow-competitor, his caddie, or his equipment, there's no penalty. Just replace the ball. **Rule 18–4.**

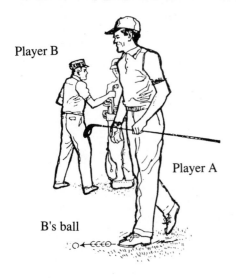

"Hey, you kicked my ball."

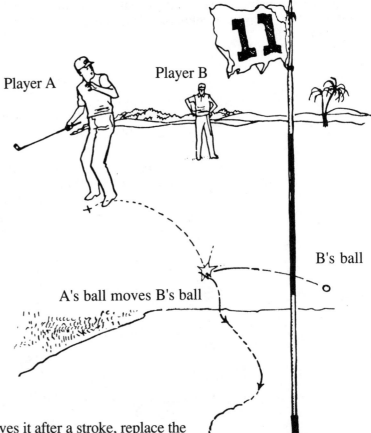

The Ball Moved by Another Ball

If a ball in play is at rest and another ball moves it after a stroke, replace the ball that was at rest. **Rule 18–5.**

Ball in Motion, Deflected, or Stopped

1. Whether in match or stroke play, if a ball is deflected or stopped by an outside agency, there's no penalty.
2. If it's done by your own caddie in match play, you lose the hole.
3. If it's done accidentally by your opponent's caddie in match play, there's no penalty and you have the option to replay.
4. In stroke play, if your own caddie stops or deflects the ball, you take a two-stroke penalty.
5. In stroke play, if your competitor's caddie stops or deflects it, there's no penalty, with some exceptions covered in the Rules.

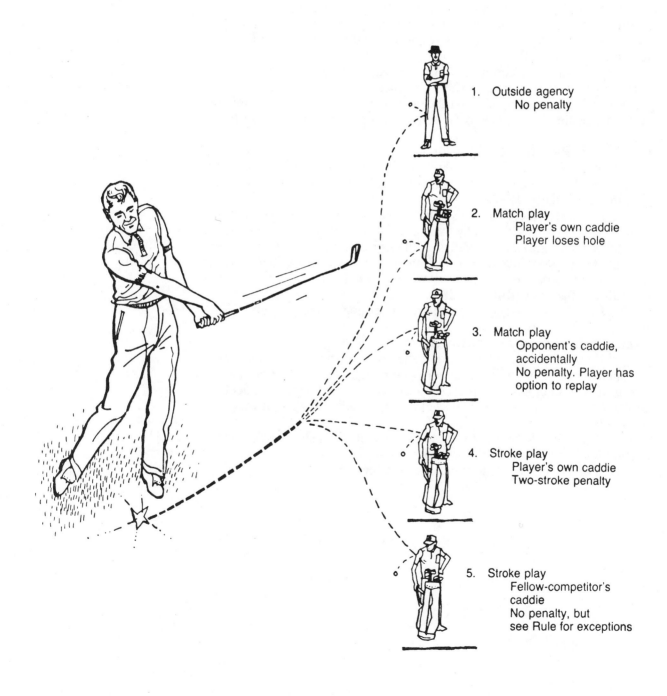

1. Outside agency
   No penalty

2. Match play
   Player's own caddie
   Player loses hole

3. Match play
   Opponent's caddie,
   accidentally
   No penalty. Player has
   option to replay

4. Stroke play
   Player's own caddie
   Two-stroke penalty

5. Stroke play
   Fellow-competitor's
   caddie
   No penalty, but
   see Rule for exceptions

By Outside Agency

If a ball in motion is accidentally deflected or stopped by any outside agency—something or someone who's not part of the game—that's a "rub of the green." There's no penalty and you play the ball as it lies.

To illustrate: You have taken a stroke and your ball is moving through the green or in a hazard; it comes to rest on a moving or animate outside agency—a porcupine, say, or a tumbleweed. You will have to *drop* the ball as close as you can to where the outside agency was when the ball came down.

On the putting green, *place* the ball as close as possible to that spot; cancel the stroke, replace the ball, and take the stroke again. By the way, worms or insects aren't big enough to count as outside agencies. If the outside agency spirits your ball away entirely and it's not recoverable, substitute another ball.

Note that if a referree or Committee says the outside agency purposely deflected your ball to help you (perhaps you trained the porcupine?), Rule 1–4 applies. (If the outside agency is a fellow competitor or caddie, Rule 1–2 applies to the fellow-competitor. **Rule 19–1a,b.**

By Player, Partner, Caddie, or Equipment

In match play, if you accidentally deflect or stop your ball, or your partner, your caddies, or any of your equipment deflects or stops it, you will lose the hole. **Rule 19–2a.**

If you stop a competitor's ball this way in stroke play, you get a penalty of two strokes, then play the ball as it lies—except if it comes to rest in your or your partner's or caddies' clothes or equipment. If this happens through the green or in a hazard, *drop* the ball as near as possible to where the article was when the ball came down on it. On the putting green, *place* the ball on that spot. **Rule 19–2b.**

Rule 20–2a covers an exception concerning a dropped ball.

Accidentally by an Opponent in Match Play

If your ball is accidentally deflected or stopped by an opponent or an opponent's caddie or equipment, there's no penalty. You play your ball as it lies, unless another stroke is played by anyone. If that happens, cancel the stroke and replay it, with the ball as close as possible to where it was originally.

See Rule 17–3b about what to do when the ball strikes someone attending a flagstick, and Rule 1–2 for what to do if the ball is purposely deflected or stopped by your opponents or their caddies.

Ball Deflected by Another Ball

If your ball is moving after your stroke and another ball at rest stops or deflects it, play your ball as it lies. However, if this happens on the putting green in stroke play—your stroked ball hits another ball that was resting on the putting green before your stroke—it's going to cost you two strokes.

   If your ball is in motion after your stroke and is deflected or stopped by another ball also in motion, there's no penalty, unless you broke Rule 16–1g, which forbids taking a stroke with another ball in motion and comes with a penalty. **Rule 19–5.**

   Remember, you may cancel and replay your stroke only when the ball is deflected by an outside agency, either object or creature.

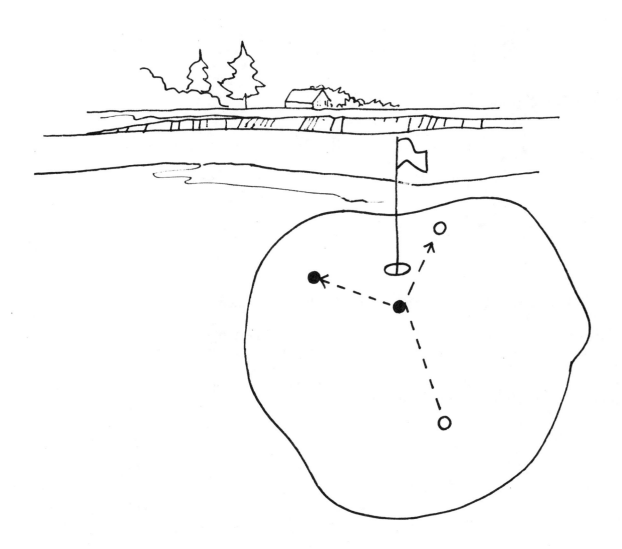

Lifting, Dropping, and Placing; Playing from the Wrong Place

When you legally lift your ball, you may do it yourself or anyone else you ask may do it. If there's any penalty, it will be yours.

If the ball is going to be replaced, make sure that whoever does it marks the spot before he or she lifts it. If it's not marked, you'll be penalized.

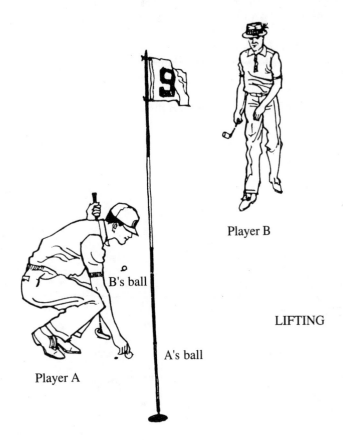

Player B

B's ball

A's ball

Player A

LIFTING

If a ball or marker is accidentally moved as the ball is being lifted, you may replace it without penalty.

To mark the ball, place a marker, or a small coin or some such, right behind the ball. If this won't work because the marker would interfere with the stance or stroke of another player, place the marker one or more clubhead-lengths to the side of the ball. Note the distance carefully so you can measure and replace it accurately. **Rule 20–1.**

Dropping and Re-dropping

Who, How, and Where

You must drop your own ball. Stand straight, hold the ball at shoulder height, and release it. If you have someone else do it, or if you don't do it correctly yourself, it will cost you a stroke. If the ball touches you, your partner, your caddies, or your equipment before or after it lands, there's no penalty but you must drop it again; there's no limit to how many times you may re-drop it for this reason.

You must drop your ball as close as you can to the spot where it was; don't move it nearer to the hole, except where a Rule permits or requires it. If you drop your ball in a hazard, it must be dropped and come to rest in the hazard.

A Dropped Ball Rolling into a New Situation

You must re-drop your ball if it rolls:

- out of a hazard;
- onto a putting green;
- out of bounds; or
- back into the situation that caused you to take relief.

Rule 24–2 or 25.

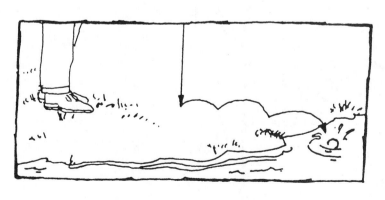

Water hazard

You must re-drop your ball if it comes to rest:

- more than two club-lengths from where it first struck after the drop, or
- nearer the hole than it was originally, unless otherwise permitted by Rule 20–2b or any other Rule.

If the ball rolls again into one of these situations, place it as close as you can to where it first struck the ground when it was re-dropped. If the ball isn't immediately recoverable, you may substitute another ball. **Rule 20–2c.**

Placing and Replacing

How and Where

You must *drop* your own ball, but either you or your partner may *place it*. A ball also may be *replaced* by you or your partner, or by whoever lifted or moved it.

If a ball or a marker is accidentally moved as you place or replace the ball, there's no penalty if the accidental movement is directly caused by the placement. You should replace them where they should be.

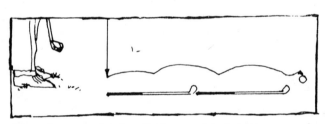

More than two club-lengths from point of striking ground

Out of bounds

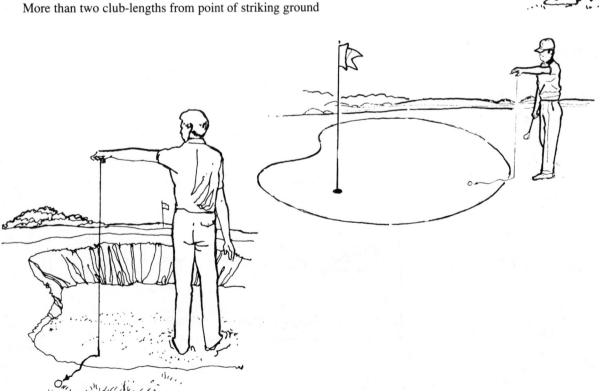

62

When the Lie of a Placed or Replaced Ball Is Altered

What do you do if the original lie of the ball to be placed or replaced is altered?

- Except in a hazard, place the ball in the nearest lie that's similar to the original lie. Don't put it more than one club-length from the original spot; don't put it nearer the hole than it was; and don't put it in a hazard.

- In a water hazard, follow all the above restrictions, but the ball must be placed in the water hazard.

- In a bunker, recreate the original lie as best you can, then place the ball in it.

Rule 20–3b.

Spot Not Determinable

If you can't tell the exact spot where the ball should be placed, you must:

- through the green, drop the ball as near as you can to where it lay, but not nearer the hole or in a hazard;

- in a hazard, drop it in the hazard as near as possible to where it lay; and

- on the putting green, place it as near as you can to its original lie, but not in a hazard. **Rule 20–3c.**

The Ball Fails to Remain on Spot

If you place the ball and it doesn't stay put, put it back with no penalty. If it still won't stay there, you should:

- place it as near to the spot as you can so it will rest, but not nearer the hole or in a hazard—unless it was in a hazard, or

- in the case of a hazard, place it at the nearest spot in the hazard where it will rest, but not nearer the hole.

When a Dropped or Placed Ball Is in Play

As soon as you drop or place your ball, it's back in play. A substituted ball is in play as soon as it is legally dropped or placed. **Rule 20–4.**

Player A

Player B

Player B

"Please lift your ball. It interferes with me."

B's lie is altered

*Playing the Next Stroke From Where the Previous Stroke Was
Played*

When you chose to legally play the next stroke from where the previous
stroke was played—or the Rules make you play it there—you must:

• on the teeing ground, play the ball from anywhere within the teeing
  ground, and if you like, tee it;
• through the green or on a hazard, drop the ball;
• on the putting green, place it. **Rule 20–5.**

*"I've hit my shot out of bounds. I'll have to put another ball in play. Do I drop it or place
it?"*

"You are through the green, so you drop it."

Lifting a Ball That Is Wrongly Dropped or Placed

A ball dropped or placed in a wrong place, or otherwise in a way that doesn't follow the Rules, may be lifted. If done correctly, there's no penalty—as long as it wasn't yet played. **Rule 20–6.**

"You dropped in the wrong place. But since you haven't played the ball you can lift it and drop correctly."

Cleaning the Ball

Rule 16–1b allows you to lift and clean your ball on the putting green, as long as you put it back where it was.

Other than on the putting green, you may clean your ball when it is legally lifted—unless you lifted it:

- to tell if it's unfit for play (Rule 5–3);
- to identify it (Rule 12–2), in which case it may be cleaned only to the extent necessary for identification; or
- because it's interfering with or assisting play (Rule 22).

If you clean your ball any other way, it will cost you a stroke and you must replace the ball. As mentioned earlier, for not replacing it when you should have, you'll be penalized according to 20–3a, but there won't be an additional penalty for violating Rule 21.

If you are penalized under Rule 5–3, 12–2, or 22, you won't get an additional penalty for Rule 21. **Rule 21.**

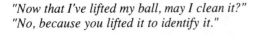

"Now that I've lifted my ball, may I clean it?"
"No, because you lifted it to identify it."

"May I remove the blade of grass from my ball?"
"No, since it adheres to your ball, it's not a loose impediment."

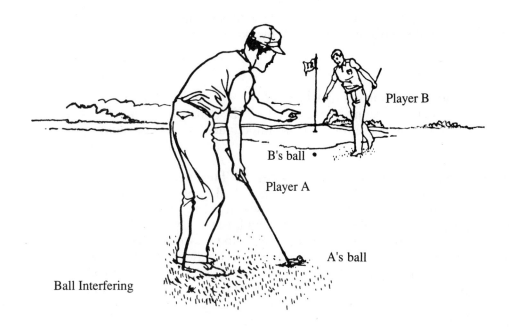

Player B

B's ball •

Player A

A's ball

Ball Interfering

Ball Interfering with or Assisting Play

You're allowed to lift your ball to help another player, or have any other ball lifted if it might interfere with your play or might assist the play of another player. But you can't do these things while another ball is in play.

In stroke play, if you're required to lift your ball, you may play first rather than lift.

In any case, replace the ball. If it's accidentally moved, there's no penalty, even if you accidentally drop it or push it aside; just replace it where it should be. **Rule 22.**

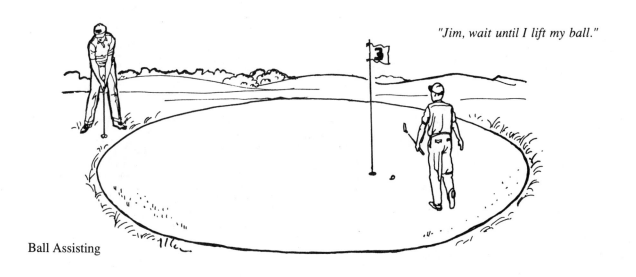

"Jim, wait until I lift my ball."

Ball Assisting

Loose Impediments

May the twig be removed? Yes, since the ball does not lie in a hazard, but there's a penalty if the ball moves, unless the ball is lying on the putting green.

Relief

Any loose impediment may be removed without penalty—except if both the ball and the impediment are in or touching a hazard. When your ball is in motion, you may not remove a loose impediment in the line of play. **Rule 23–1.**

Ball Moving After Loose Impediment Is Touched

While you're through the green, if your ball moves after a loose impediment lying within a club-length of it was touched by you, your partner, or your caddies, but before you've addressed it, you will get a penalty stroke for moving the ball. You must then replace the ball, unless its movement began after you started to swing and you didn't stop your swing.

On the putting green, if the ball or marker moves while any loose impediment is being moved, replace it. There's no penalty as long as the movement of the ball was a direct cause of moving the loose impediment. **Rule 18–2c.**

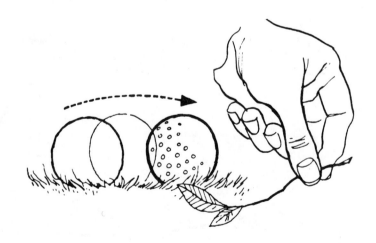

Obstructions

Movable Obstructions

Here's how you may obtain relief from a movable object:

- If the ball doesn't lie in or on the obstruction, move the obstruction. If the ball moves, there's no penalty as long as your moving the obstruction was the direct cause of the ball moving. If not, you'll be penalized under Rule 18–2a. You should also replace the ball.

- If the ball is in or on the obstruction, lift it and move the obstruction. Then, through the green or in a hazard, drop the ball. On the putting green, place it. Always put the ball as close as possible to a point directly under where it was lying in or on the obstruction. Don't place it nearer to the hole than it was.

You're allowed to clean the ball when you lift it; you're not allowed to move obstructions—except for the flagstick and players' equipment—out of your ball's way when your ball is in motion. **Rule 24–1.**

Immovable Obstructions

Interference

An immovable obstructions is "interfering" when the ball lies in or on the obstruction. It's also interference when the ball lies so close to the obstruction that it disrupts the player's stance or the area of intended swing.

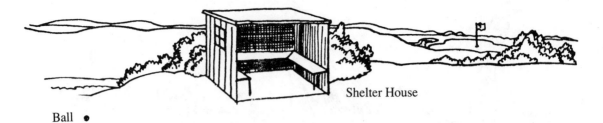

Shelter House

Ball •

If a player's ball lies on the putting green, the obstruction is "interfering" if it is intervening in the line of putt. Other than when you're on the putting green, simply being in the line of play is not interference.

For instance, in the illustration the ball is far enough behind the shelter house that it doesn't interfere with the player's swing. Because it's only in the player's line of play, no relief and no ball dropping are allowed.

Relief

Except when the ball lies in or touches a water hazard or lateral water hazard, you may obtain relief from an immovable object as follows:

• If you are through the green, determine a point that is the nearest point to the ball's lie, does not bring the ball nearer to the hole, avoids the interference, and is not in a hazard or on a putting green. In determining this point, you may not cross over, through, or under the obstruction.

Lift and drop the ball within one club-length of this point.

Note that you may cross over, through, or under the obstruction if the ball lies in or under it, or if the obstruction is the artificial surface of a road or a path.

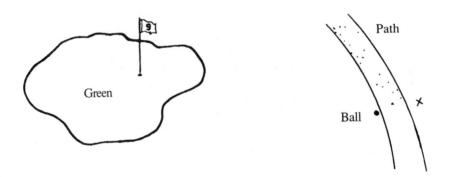

In the illustration, for instance, the player's stance is obstructed by the paved cart path. In this case, the player may cross the path in obtaining relief. He must drop the ball within a club-length of point X, which is the nearest point not closer to the hole.

• If your ball lies in or touches a bunker, the procedure is the same as through the green—but make sure the ball is dropped in the bunker.

• On the putting green, lift the ball and place it on the spot nearest to where it was, while avoiding the interference. In a hazard, don't put the ball nearer to the hole than it was. You may clean it.

See Rule 20–2c about what to do if your ball again rolls into the position from which you were originally seeking relief.

You may not obtain relief if the interference of something besides the immovable obstruction would prevent you from taking the stroke anyway, or if the immovable obstruction would be interfering only if you took an abnormal stance, swing, or direction of play. You also can't obtain relief if the ball lies in or touches a water or lateral water hazard. You must play it as it lies or proceed as described in Rule 26–1. **Rule 24–2b.**

Ball Lost

If there's reasonable evidence that a ball is lost in an immovable obstruction, there's no penalty for substituting another ball; follow the steps described above under "Relief" (Rule 24–2b). The ball's lie will be the place where it entered the obstruction. If the ball is lost in an underground drain pipe or a culvert that has its entrance in a hazard, you must drop the ball in the hazard or take the steps in Rule 26–1, if that's legal in your case. **Rule 24–c.**

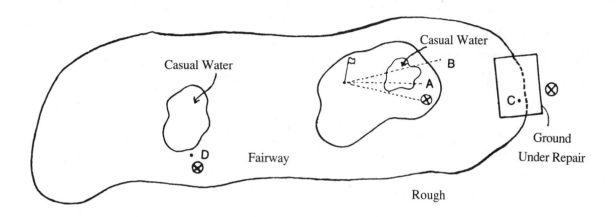

Abnormal Ground Conditions and the Wrong Putting Green

Relief From Casual Water or Ground Under Repair

Interference occurs anytime your ball lies in or touches casual water, ground under repair, or the hole, cast, or runway of an animal. If your ball's on the putting green, any of these conditions in the line of your putt is interference. When there's interference, you may either play the ball as it lies or take relief in one of the following ways:

On the Putting Green

In the illustration, Ball A lies on the putting green, with casual water standing between it and the hole. This ball may be lifted and placed on the X, without penalty. As always, X is the nearest point to the ball's original position that gives the most relief from the casual water, but won't put the ball nearer to the hole. If Ball A were lying *in* the casual water on the putting green, a similar action could be taken. **Rule 25–1b (iii).**

However, Ball B lies off the putting green, and therefore the player may not obtain relief from the casual water that's on the green between the ball and the hole.

Through the Green

Ball C lies in ground under repair, in an area that is normally the fairway. Here, the player may lift Ball C and drop it outside the ground under repair without penalty. You must drop it within one club-length of the nearby X, which here is not nearer the hole, avoids interference by the ground under repair, and is not in a hazard or on a putting green. The permissible drop area for Ball C is in the rough. However, please note that the Rules don't distinguish between fairway and rough—both are "through the green." **Rule 25–1b(i).**

Ball D lies so near to casual water that a right-handed player would be forced to stand in the casual water. The player may, therefore, lift and drop the ball without penalty. It must be dropped outside the casual water, within one club-length of the nearest point of relief not nearer the hole, on the X. **Rule 25–1b(ii).**

Casual Water in a Bunker

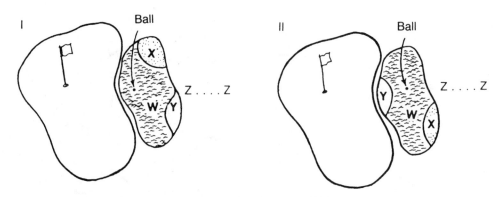

In the illustration, the area marked W is three-inch-deep water; area X is an eighth of an inch deep; area Y has no casual water.

In scenario I, the player would probably like to drop the ball in area X. However, he has only two legal options:

- to drop it in the nearest point in area Y, without penalty;
- to drop it along the Z . . . Z line, with a one-stroke penalty.

In scenario II, the player may not drop the ball in area Y, because that would mean moving the ball closer to the hole than it was. He may drop the ball only:

- at the nearest point in area X, with no penalty; or
- along line Z . . . Z with a one-stroke penalty.

In a bunker, if there's interference by casual water, ground under repair, or an animal's hole, runway, etc., you may:

- without penalty lift and drop the ball as close as possible to where it was, on ground that gives the best relief but doesn't bring your ball nearer to the hole;
- with a one-stroke penalty drop your ball outside the bunker. Make sure to keep the spot where your ball *was* lying directly between the hole and the spot where you drop it.

Ball Lost in Casual Water or Ground Under Repair

Before you may say your ball is lost and act accordingly, there's got to be some evidence to that effect. If it *is* lost, here's how you may take relief:

First, determine the point closest to where the ball crossed into the water or ground that:

- doesn't move the ball nearer to the hole;
- avoids the interference; and
- is not in a hazard or on a putting green.

Without penalty, drop your ball within one club-length of that point.

"I'm sure my ball went in here, but I can't find it."

Embedded Ball

A ball embedded in its own pitch-mark in any closely mown area through the green may be lifted, cleaned, and dropped without penalty. It must be dropped as close as possible to where it was lying, but not any closer to the hole. The term "closely mown area" includes any part of the course, including paths through the rough that have been mown to the height of the fairway, or shorter. **Rule 25–2.**

Ball in fairway   Ball in rough

Ball on the Wrong Putting Green

If your ball lies on the wrong putting green (a green other than the one on the hole you're playing), you must first determine the point closest to where your ball lies that doesn't move the ball nearer to the hole and is not in a hazard or on a putting green.

Then, without penalty, lift and drop your ball within one club-length of this point. In the illustration, the player must drop his ball off the green within one club-length of point X. **Rule 25–3.**

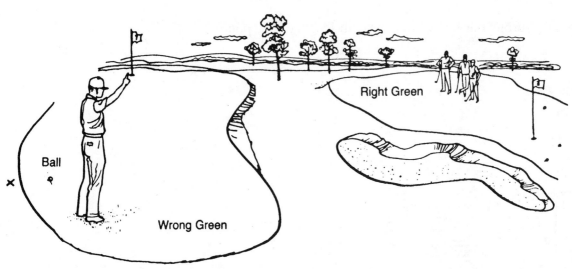

"May I drop it up at that end so I won't have to play over the bunker?"

Water Hazards (Including Lateral Water Hazards)

A Ball in a Water Hazard—Procedure

The brook between A–A and B–B is a lateral water hazard; other parts of the brook are regular water hazards. C and D are the spots where balls last crossed the edge of the hazards.

In the diagram, Player T's ball is in the brook (the water hazard) in front of the green. He has two choices, both of which come with a one-stroke penalty:

- He may drop the ball behind the water hazard. However, the player must make sure that the point where the original ball crossed the edge of the water hazard (C) stays directly between the hole and the spot where he drops the new ball. There's no limit to how far back from the brook he may drop the ball (X–X–X–X–X . . .). **Rule 26–1b.**
- He may drop the ball as near as possible to the spot where the original ball was played. If the stroke was played from the teeing ground, the player may tee the ball anywhere within the teeing ground. **Rule 26–1a.**

In the same diagram, player Q's ball has entered the lateral water hazard at the left. Player Q has three choices, all of which include a one-stroke penalty.

- She may drop a ball behind the lateral water hazard. She must keep the point where the original ball crossed the edge of the water hazard directly between the hole and the spot where she drops the new ball. There's no limit to how far behind the lateral water hazard she may drop the ball (line Z–Z–Z–Z . . .). **Rule 26–1c.**

- She may drop a ball as close as possible to where the original ball was played. If the stroke was taken from the teeing ground, she may tee anywhere on the teeing ground. **Rule 26–1a.**

- She may drop a ball outside the hazard. It must be within two club-lengths of the point (D) where the ball crossed the edge of the hazard, or a point on the opposite edge of the hazard, equidistant from the hole. The ball must be dropped and come to rest no nearer to the hole than point D. In the diagram, area E shows where, on either side of the brook, Q may drop her ball. **Rule 26–1c.**

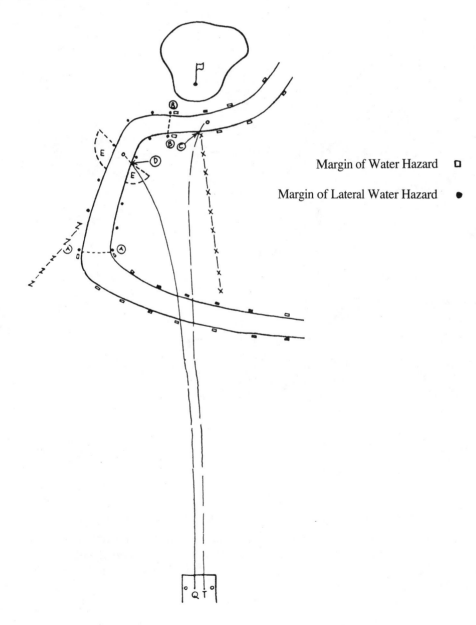

Margin of Water Hazard   ▫

Margin of Lateral Water Hazard   ●

Doubt About Whether the Ball Is in the Water Hazard

If you stroke your ball in the direction of a water hazard and then can't find it, you can't just assume it's lost. There must be some kind of evidence that it actually is lost in the water and not elsewhere. Without that evidence, it must be considered to be just lost and not lost in a water hazard.

"If my ball is lost in the water hazard, I can save distance."

Ball Played Within a Water Hazard

When the Ball Comes to Rest in a Hazard

Sometimes it is possible to play a ball from within a water hazard—obviously, the water is not over your head and the ball is not lost. If you do play your ball from within the hazard and it comes back to rest in the hazard again, you have two options:

1.   You may play a ball as close as possible to the spot where you took your last stroke from outside the hazard. This comes with a one-stroke penalty. **Rule 20–5.**

2.   You may choose to proceed under Rule 26–1, described above. If you choose Rule 26–1 and elect under that Rule to play a ball from as close as possible to where you last played, you may then further choose not to play that dropped ball but instead to do one of the following (each with an additional one-stroke penalty):

- drop the ball behind the water hazard exactly as described above;
- only if your ball is in, touches, or is lost in a lateral water hazard may you drop a ball according to the dictates spelled out in Player Q's third option described in the diagram;
- play a ball as close as possible to the spot where you took your last stroke outside the hazard.

When the Ball Is Lost or Unplayable Outside the Hazard or Out of Bounds
If you play a ball from within a water hazard and it becomes lost, unplayable outside the hazard, or out of bounds you may, with a one-stroke penalty:

- play a ball as close (in the hazard) to where the original ball was played;
- or, with an additional one-stroke penalty, proceed under Rule 26–1b or 26–1c. Use as a reference point the spot where the original ball last crossed the edge of the hazard before it came to rest in the hazard;
- or, with an additional one-stroke penalty, play your next stroke as close as you can from the spot where you took your last stroke from outside the hazard.

Note that if a ball played from within a water hazard is unplayable outside the hazard, nothing in Rule 26–2b stops you from proceeding under Rule 28b,c. **Rule 26–2.**

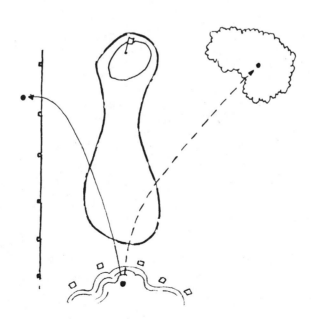

Balls That Are Lost, Out of Bounds, and Unplayable

Ball Lost or Out of Bounds

Out of Bounds

In the diagram, Player A's ball is out of bounds. He must replay from the tee, count both strokes made, and add a penalty stroke to the score for the hole. **Rule 27–1.**

Lost

Player B can't find her ball in the thick underbrush. She must play again from the tee, count both strokes, *and* add a penalty stroke to her score for the hole. **Rule 27–1.**

Provisional Ball

If it's possible that a ball just played may be lost outside a water hazard or may have gone out of bounds, you're allowed to play a provisional ball. You must play it as nearly as possible from the spot where you played the original ball. In match play, you must inform your opponent, and in stroke play your marker or fellow-competitor, that you intend to play this provisional ball. Also, you must play it before you or your partner starts forward to search for the original ball. If you don't do these things, your provisional ball will automatically become the ball in play. The original ball is then "lost" whether or not you find it, and you have a one-stroke penalty. **Rule 27–2.**

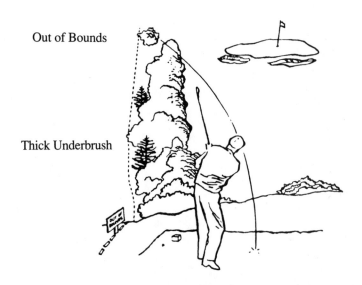

Out of Bounds

Thick Underbrush

"That may be lost or out of bounds. I'll play a provisional."

POND

"That could be unplayable in the pond. Is a provisional allowed?"
"Sorry—not for that reason."

When a Provisional Ball Becomes a Ball in Play

Go on playing with the provisional ball until you reach the place where you think the original ball may be. If you play a stroke from that place or from a place closer than there to the hole, the original ball is considered lost and the provisional ball becomes the ball in play. You must also take a one-stroke penalty.

If the original ball is lost outside a water hazard or is out of bounds, the provisional ball becomes the ball in play, again with a one-stroke penalty. **Rule 27–2b.**

However, if your first ball isn't lost, in a water hazard, or out of bounds, then abandon the provisional ball and continue with the original one. If you fail to reinstate the original ball into play, any further strokes you play with the provisional one will be played with a wrong ball. **Rule 27–2c.**

Original ball

Provisional ball

"That puts the provisional ball in play."

"That's unplayable. I'll have to give up the provisional ball, too."

Original ball

Provisional ball

An Unplayable Ball

In the diagram, Player C finds his ball at the base of a thick, bushy tree. He declares it to be unplayable under Rule 28, which allows players to declare balls unplayable anywhere except when the ball lies in or touches a water hazard. Now he has two options: He may play again from the tee with a one-stroke penalty, or, he may drop a ball, also with a one-stroke penalty, either

- within two club-lengths of the point where the ball lay, but no nearer to the hole, shown by the shaded area marked Z, or

- behind the unplayable lie on line XXX, making sure to keep the point where the ball was unplayable directly between the hole and the spot where the ball is dropped.

If the ball lies in a bunker, the player may proceed under either of the options above. However, if he chooses the last one he must drop in the bunker. **Rule 28.**

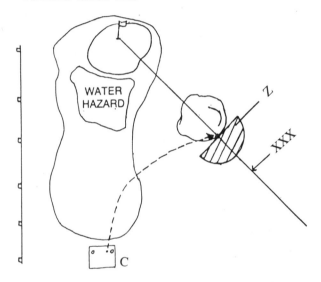

Other Forms of Play

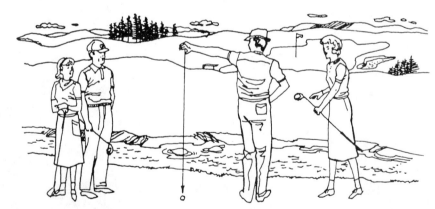

Threesomes and Foursomes

The woman has hit the ball into the water hazard and she and her partner wish to drop a ball behind the hazard under penalty of one stroke (Rule 26–1). Who should play the next stroke, the man or his partner?

In this case, the man must play the next stroke because a penalty stroke does not affect the order of play.

General

In a threesome or a foursome playing a stipulated round, the partners must play alternately from the teeing grounds and during the play of each hole. For instance, in a foursome, you would play, then an opponent, then your partner, then the other opponent. Penalty strokes don't affect the order of play. **Rule 29-1.**

Match Play

If you play when it's your partner's turn, you lose the hole. **Rule 29-2.**

Stroke Play

If you or your partner plays a stroke out of order, the stroke is canceled and you get a two-stroke penalty. Then you must set things right by playing a ball in the correct order at the spot where it was first played out of order. If you then play a stroke from the next teeing ground without first correcting the earlier error, or leave the putting green without declaring your intention to correct the error, you and your partner will be disqualified. **Rule 29-3.**

"My partner's not here, so I'll represent our side."

Four-Ball Match and Stroke Play

Representation of Side

You alone or your partner alone may play for your side for a part of a match or round. An absent partner may join a match between holes, but not during a hole. **Rule 30-3a, 31-2.**

Order of Play

Match Play and Stroke Play
        You and your partner may play your balls in whatever order you
think is best for you. **Rules   30–3c, 31–5.**

"You putt first, partner, so I can get some idea about the line."

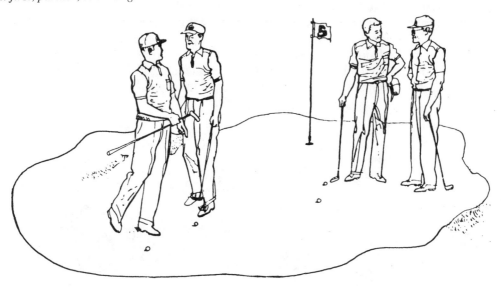

A Breach of Rules That Affects Other Players

If you break a Rule and as a result your partner is assisted in his or her play,
or if it hurts an opponent's play, you and your partner will both be
penalized. **Rules   30–3f and 31–8.**

"You're not allowed to remove loose impediments in a hazard. We are both penalized."

The Committee

Combining Match and Stroke Play Prohibited

Some stroke-play Rules differ so fundamentally from match-play Rules that the two games cannot—and may not, by the Rules—be combined. Any results from matches that attempt such a combination, and their scores, will not be accepted. **Rule 33–1.**

"Can't we kill two birds with one stone today—play our match in the club championship and also compete in the weekly stroke play?"

"No, it wouldn't be right."

Defining Bounds and Margins

It is the Committee that defines:

- the course and out of bounds;
- the margins of water hazards and lateral water hazards;
- ground under repair; and
- obstructions and integral parts of the course. **Rule 33–2a.**

"Am I in a water hazard or not?"

An Unplayable Course

If the Committee or its representative declares the course to be unplayable, it may temporarily suspend match or stroke play. It may also, in stroke play, void the play altogether and cancel all scores.

When play is temporarily suspended, it must be resumed from where it was discontinued, even if on a later day. When a round is canceled, all penalties of that round are canceled. **Rule 33–2d.**

Local Rules That Waive Penalties

Local Rules are not allowed to waive the penalties of the Rules of Golf. **Rule 33–8b.**

"There's a Local Rule here—no penalty for dropping out of a water hazard. That's wrong."

THE RULES OF GOLF

Section I
ETIQUETTE

Courtesy on the Course

Safety

Prior to playing a stroke or making a practice swing, the player should ensure that no one is standing close by or in a position to be hit by the club, the ball or any stones, pebbles, twigs or the like which may be moved by the stroke or swing.

Consideration for Other Players

The player who has the honor should be allowed to play before his opponent or fellow-competitor tees his ball.

No one should move, talk or stand close to or directly behind the ball or the hole when a player is addressing the ball or making a stroke.

In the interest of all, players should play without delay.

No player should play until the players in front are out of range.

Players searching for a ball should signal the players behind them to pass as soon as it becomes apparent that the ball will not easily be found. They should not search for five minutes before doing so. They should not continue play until the players following them have passed and are out of range.

When the play of a hole has been completed, players should immediately leave the putting green.

Priority on the Course

In the absence of special rules, two-ball matches should have precedence over and be entitled to pass any three- or four-ball match, which should invite them through.

A single player has no standing and should give way to a match of any kind.

Any match playing a whole round is entitled to pass a match playing a shorter round.

If a match fails to keep its place on the course and loses more than one clear hole on the players in front, it should invite the match following to pass.

Care of the Course

Holes in Bunkers

Before leaving a bunker, a player should carefully fill up and smooth over all holes and footprints made by him.

Replace Divots; Repair Ball-Marks and Damage by Spikes

Through the green, a player should ensure that any turf cut or displaced by him is replaced at once and pressed down and that any damage to the putting green made by a ball is carefully repaired. Damage to the putting green caused by golf shoe spikes should be repaired *on completion of the hole.*

Damage to Greens — Flagsticks, Bags, etc.

Players should ensure that, when putting down bags or the flagstick, no damage is done to the putting green and that neither they nor their caddies damage the hole by standing close to it, in handling the flagstick or in removing the ball from the hole. The flagstick should be properly replaced in the hole before the players leave the putting green. Players should not damage the putting green by leaning on their putters, particularly when removing the ball from the hole.

Golf Carts

Local notices regulating the movement of golf carts should be strictly observed.

Damage Through Practice Swings

In taking practice swings, players should avoid causing damage to the course, particularly the tees, by removing divots.

Section II
DEFINITIONS

Addressing the Ball

A player has "addressed the ball" when he has taken his stance and has also grounded his club, except that in a hazard a player has addressed the ball when he has taken his stance.

Advice

"Advice" is any counsel or suggestion which could influence a player in determining his play, the choice of a club or the method of making a stroke.

Information on the Rules or on matters of public information, such as the position of hazards or the flagstick on the putting green, is not advice.

Ball Deemed to Move

See "Move or Moved."

Ball Holed

See "Holed."

Ball Lost

See "Lost Ball."

Ball in Play

A ball is "in play" as soon as the player has made a stroke on the teeing ground. It remains in play until holed out, except when it is lost, out of bounds or lifted, or another ball has been substituted under an applicable Rule, whether or not such Rule permits substitution; a ball so substituted becomes the ball in play.

Bunker

A "bunker" is a hazard consisting of a prepared area of ground, often a hollow, from which turf or soil has been removed and replaced with sand or the like. Grass-covered ground bordering or within a bunker is not part of the bunker. The margin of a bunker extends vertically downwards, but not upwards.

Caddie

A "caddie" is one who carries or handles a player's clubs during play and otherwise assists him in accordance with the Rules.

When one caddie is employed by more than one player, he is always deemed to be the caddie of the player whose ball is involved, and equipment carried by him is deemed to be that player's equipment, except when the caddie acts upon specific directions of another player, in which case he is considered to be that other player's caddie.

Casual Water

"Casual water" is any temporary accumulation of water on the course which is visible before or after the player takes his stance and is not in a water hazard. Snow and natural ice, other than frost, are either casual water or loose impediments, at the option of the player. Manufactured ice is an obstruction. Dew and frost are not casual water.

Committee

The "Committee" is the committee in charge of the competition or, if the matter does not arise in a competition, the committee in charge of the course.

Competitor

A "competitor" is a player in a stroke competition. A "fellow-competitor" is any person with whom the competitor plays. Neither is partner of the other.

In stroke play foursome and four-ball competitions, where the context so admits, the word "competitor" or "fellow-competitor" includes his partner.

Course

The "course" is the whole area within which play is permitted. See Rule 33-2.

Equipment

"Equipment" is anything used, worn or carried by or for the player except any ball he has played at the hole being played and any small object, such as a coin or a tee, when used to mark the position of a ball or the extent of an area in which a ball is to be dropped. Equipment includes a golf cart, whether or not motorized. If such a cart is shared by two or more players, the cart and everything in it are deemed to be the equipment of the player whose ball is involved except that, when the cart is being moved by one of the players sharing it, the cart and everything in it are deemed to be that player's equipment.

Note: A ball played at the hole being played is equipment when it has been lifted and not put back into play.

Fellow-Competitor

See "Competitor."

Flagstick

The "flagstick" is a movable straight indicator, with or without bunting or other material attached, centered in the hole to show its position. It shall be circular in cross-section.

Forecaddie

A "forecaddie" is one who is employed by the Committee to indicate to players the position of balls during play. He is an outside agency.

Ground Under Repair

"Ground under repair" is any portion of the course so marked by order of the Committee or so declared by its authorized representative. It includes material piled for removal and a hole made by a greenkeeper, even if not so marked. Stakes and lines defining ground under repair are in such ground. The margin of ground under repair extends vertically downwards, but not upwards.

Note 1: Grass cuttings and other material left on the course which have been abandoned and are not intended to be removed are not ground under repair unless so marked.

Note 2: The Committee may make a Local Rule prohibiting play from ground under repair.

Hazards

A "hazard" is any bunker or water hazard.

Hole

The "hole" shall be 4¼ inches (108mm) in diameter and at least 4 inches (100mm) deep. If a lining is used, it shall be sunk at least 1 inch (25mm) below the putting green surface unless the nature of the soil makes it impracticable to do so; its outer diameter shall not exceed 4¼ inches (108mm).

Holed

A ball is "holed" when it is at rest within the circumference of the hole and all of it is below the level of the lip of the hole.

Honor

The side entitled to play first from the teeing ground is said to have the "honor."

Lateral Water Hazard

A "lateral water hazard" is a water hazard or that part of a water hazard so situated that it is not possible or is deemed by the Committee to be impracticable to drop a ball behind the water hazard in accordance with Rule 26-1b.

That part of a water hazard to be played as a lateral water hazard should be distinctively marked.

Note: Lateral water hazards should be defined by red stakes or lines.

Line of Play

The "line of play" is the direction which the player wishes his ball to take after a stroke, plus a reasonable distance on either side of the intended direction. The line of play extends vertically upwards from the ground, but does not extend beyond the hole.

Line of Putt

The "line of putt" is the line which the player wishes his ball to take after a stroke on the putting green. Except with respect to Rule 16-1e, the line of putt includes a reasonable distance on either side of the intended line. The line of putt does not extend beyond the hole.

Loose Impediments

"Loose impediments" are natural objects such as stones, leaves, twigs, branches and the like, dung, worms and insects and casts or heaps made by them, provided they are not fixed or growing, are not solidly embedded and do not adhere to the ball.

Sand and loose soil are loose impediments on the putting green, but not elsewhere.

Snow and natural ice, other than frost, are either casual water or loose impediments, at the option of the player. Manufactured ice is an obstruction.

Dew and frost are not loose impediments.

Lost Ball

A ball is "lost" if:

a. It is not found or identified as his by the player within five minutes after the player's side or his or their caddies have begun to search for it; or

b. The player has put another ball into play under the Rules, even though he may not have searched for the original ball; or

c. The player has played any stroke with a provisional ball from the place where the original ball is likely to be or from a point nearer the hole than that place, whereupon the provisional ball becomes the ball in play.

Time spent in playing a wrong ball is not counted in the five-minute period allowed for search.

Marker

A "marker" is one who is appointed by the Committee to record a competitor's score in stroke play. He may be a fellow-competitor. He is not a referee.

Matches

See "Sides and Matches."

Move or Moved

A ball is deemed to have "moved" if it leaves its position and comes to rest in any other place.

Observer

An "observer" is one who is appointed by the Committee to assist a referee to decide questions of fact and to report to him any breach of a Rule. An observer should not attend the flagstick, stand at or mark the position of the hole, or lift the ball or mark its position.

Obstructions

An "obstruction" is anything artificial, including the artificial surfaces and sides of roads and paths and manufactured ice, except:

a. Objects defining out of bounds, such as walls, fences, stakes and railings;

b. Any part of an immovable artificial object which is out of bounds; and

c. Any construction declared by the Committee to be an integral part of the course.

Out of Bounds

"Out of bounds" is ground on which play is prohibited.

When out of bounds is defined by reference to stakes or a fence or as being beyond stakes or a fence, the out of bounds line is determined by the nearest inside points of the stakes or fence posts at ground level excluding angled supports.

When out of bounds is defined by a line on the ground, the line itself is out of bounds.

The out of bounds line extends vertically upwards and downwards.

A ball is out of bounds when all of it lies out of bounds.

A player may stand out of bounds to play a ball lying within bounds.

Outside Agency

An "outside agency" is any agency not part of the match or, in stroke play, not part of the competitor's side, and includes a referee, a marker, an observer or a fore-caddie. Neither wind nor water is an outside agency.

Partner

A "partner" is a player associated with another player on the same side.

In a threesome, foursome, best-ball or four-ball match, where the context so admits, the word "player" includes his partner or partners.

Penalty Stroke

A "penalty stroke" is one added to the score of a player or side under certain Rules. In a threesome or foursome, penalty strokes do not affect the order of play.

Provisional Ball

A "provisional ball" is a ball played under Rule 27-2 for a ball which may be lost outside a water hazard or may be out of bounds.

Putting Green

The "putting green" is all ground of the hole being played which is specially prepared for putting or otherwise defined as such by the Committee. A ball is on the putting green when any part of it touches the putting green.

Referee

A "referee" is one who is appointed by the Committee to accompany players to decide questions of fact and apply the Rules of Golf. He shall act on any breach of a Rule which he observes or is reported to him.

A referee should not attend the flagstick, stand at or mark the position of the hole, or lift the ball or mark its position.

Rub of the Green

A "rub of the green" occurs when a ball in motion is accidentally deflected or stopped by any outside agency (see Rule 19-1).

Rule

The term "Rule" includes Local Rules made by the Committee under Rule 33-8a.

Sides and Matches

Side: A player, or two or more players who are partners.

Single: A match in which one plays against another.

Threesome: A match in which one plays against two, and each side plays one ball.

Foursome: A match in which two play against two, and each side plays one ball.

Three-Ball: A match play competition in which three play against one another, each playing his own ball. Each player is playing two distinct matches.

Best-Ball: A match in which one plays against the better ball of two or the best ball of three players.

Four-Ball: A match in which two play their better ball against the better ball of two other players.

Stance

Taking the "stance" consists in a player placing his feet in position for and preparatory to making a stroke.

Stipulated Round

The "stipulated round" consists of playing the holes of the course in their correct sequence unless otherwise

authorized by the Committee. The number of holes in a stipulated round is 18 unless a smaller number is authorized by the Committee. As to extension of stipulated round in match play, see Rule 2-3.

Stroke

A "stroke" is the forward movement of the club made with the intention of fairly striking at and moving the ball, but if a player checks his downswing voluntarily before the clubhead reaches the ball he is deemed not to have made a stroke.

Teeing Ground

The "teeing ground" is the starting place for the hole to be played. It is a rectangular area two club-lengths in depth, the front and the sides of which are defined by the outside limits of two tee-markers. A ball is outside the teeing ground when all of it lies outside the teeing ground.

Through the Green

"Through the green" is the whole area of the course except:

a. The teeing ground and putting green of the hole being played; and

b. All hazards on the course.

Water Hazard

A "water hazard" is any sea, lake, pond, river, ditch, surface drainage ditch or other open water course (whether or not containing water) and anything of a similar nature.

All ground or water within the margin of a water hazard is part of the water hazard. The margin of a water hazard extends vertically upwards and downwards. Stakes and lines defining the margins of water hazards are in the hazards.

Note: Water hazards (other than lateral water hazards) should be defined by yellow stakes or lines.

Wrong Ball

A "wrong ball" is any ball other than:

a. The ball in play,

b. A provisional ball or

c. In stroke play, a second ball played under Rule 3-3 or Rule 20-7b.

Note: Ball in play includes a ball substituted for the ball in play when the player is proceeding under an applicable Rule which does not permit substitution.

Section III
THE RULES OF PLAY

THE GAME
Rule 1. The Game

1-1. General

The Game of Golf consists in playing a ball from the teeing ground into the hole by a stroke or successive strokes in accordance with the Rules.

No player or caddie shall take any action to influence the position or the movement of a ball except in accordance with the Rules.

PENALTY FOR BREACH OF RULE 1-2:
Match play — Loss of hole; Stroke play — Two strokes.

Note: In the case of a serious breach of Rule 1-2, the Committee may impose a penalty of disqualification.

1-3. Agreement to Waive Rules

Players shall not agree to exclude the operation of any Rule or to waive any penalty incurred.

Match play — Disqualification of both sides; Stroke play — Disqualification of competitors concerned.

(Agreeing to play out of turn in stroke play — see Rule 10-2c.)

1-4. Points Not Covered by Rules
If any point in dispute is not covered by the Rules, the decision shall be made in accordance with equity.

Rule 2. Match Play

2-1. Winner of Hole; Reckoning of Holes
In match play the game is played by holes.

Except as otherwise provided in the Rules, a hole is won by the side which holes its ball in the fewer strokes. In a handicap match the lower net score wins the hole.

The reckoning of holes is kept by the terms: so many "holes up" or "all square," and so many "to play."

A side is "dormie" when it is as many holes up as there are holes remaining to be played.

2-2. Halved Hole
A hole is halved if each side holes out in the same number of strokes.

When a player has holed out and his opponent has been left with a stroke for the half, if the player thereafter incurs a penalty, the hole is halved.

2-3. Winner of Match
A match (which consists of a stipulated round, unless otherwise decreed by the Committee) is won by the side which is leading by a number of holes greater than the number of holes remaining to be played.

The Committee may, for the purpose of settling a tie, extend the stipulated round to as many holes as are required for a match to be won.

2-4. Concession of Next Stroke, Hole or Match
When the opponent's ball is at rest or is deemed to be at rest under Rule 16-2, the player may concede the opponent to have holed out with his next stroke and the ball may be removed by either side with a club or otherwise.

A player may concede a hole or a match at any time prior to the conclusion of the hole or the match.

Concession of a stroke, hole or match may not be declined or withdrawn.

2-5. Claims
In match play, if a doubt or dispute arises between the players and no duly authorized representative of the Committee is available within a reasonable time, the players shall continue the match without delay. Any claim, if it is to be considered by the Committee, must be made before any player in the match plays from the next teeing ground or, in the case of the last hole of the match, before all players in the match leave the putting green.

No later claim shall be considered unless it is based on facts previously unknown to the player making the claim and the player making the claim had been given wrong information (Rules 6-2a and 9) by an opponent. In any case, no later claim shall be considered after the result of the match has been officially announced, unless the Committee is satisfied that the opponent knew he was giving wrong information.

2-6. General Penalty
The penalty for a breach of a Rule in match play is loss of hole except when otherwise provided.

Rule 3. Stroke Play

3-1. Winner
The competitor who plays the stipulated round or rounds in the fewest strokes is the winner.

3-2. Failure to Hole Out
If a competitor fails to hole out at any hole and does not correct his mistake before he plays a stroke from the next teeing ground or, in the case of the last hole of the round, before he leaves the putting green, *he shall be disqualified.*

3-3. Doubt as to Procedure
a. PROCEDURE
In stroke play only, when during play of a hole a competitor is doubtful of his rights or procedure, he may, without penalty, play a second ball. After the situation which caused the doubt has arisen, the competitor should, before taking further action, announce to his marker or a fellow-competitor his decision to invoke this Rule and the ball with which he will score if the Rules permit.

The competitor shall report the facts to the Committee before returning his score card unless he scores the same with both balls; if he fails to do so, *he shall be disqualified.*

b. DETERMINATION OF SCORE FOR HOLE
If the Rules allow the procedure selected in advance by the competitor, the score with the ball selected shall be his score for the hole.

If the competitor fails to announce in advance his decision to invoke this Rule or his selection, the score with the original ball or, if the original ball is not one of the balls being played, the first ball put into play shall count if the Rules allow the procedure adopted for such ball.

Note: A second ball played under Rule 3-3 is not a provisional ball under Rule 27-2.

3-4. Refusal to Comply with a Rule
If a competitor refuses to comply with a Rule affecting the rights of another competitor, *he shall be disqualified.*

3-5. General Penalty
The penalty for a breach of a Rule in stroke play is two strokes except when otherwise provided.

CLUBS AND THE BALL
The United States Golf Association and the Royal and Ancient Golf Club of St. Andrews reserve the right to change the Rules and make and change the interpretations relating to clubs, balls and other implements at any time.

Rule 4. Clubs
If there may be any reasonable basis for doubt as to whether a club which is to be manufactured conforms with Rule 4 and Appendix II, the manufacturer should submit a sample to the United States Golf Association for a ruling, such sample to become its property for reference purposes. If a manufacturer fails to do so, he assumes the risk of a ruling that the club does not conform with the Rules of Golf.

A player in doubt as to the conformity of a club should consult the United States Golf Association.

4-1. Form and Make of Clubs
A club is an implement designed to be used for striking the ball.

A putter is a club designed primarily for use on the putting green.

The player's clubs shall conform with the provisions of this Rule and with the specifications and interpretations set forth in Appendix II.

a. GENERAL
The club shall be composed of a shaft and a head. All parts of the club shall be fixed so that the club is one unit. The club shall not be designed to be adjustable except for weight. The club shall not be substantially different from the traditional and customary form and make.
(See also Appendix II.)

b. SHAFT
The shaft shall be generally straight, with the same bending and twisting properties in any direction, and

shall be attached to the clubhead at the heel either directly or through a single plain neck or socket. A putter shaft may be attached to any point in the head.

c. Grip
The grip consists of that part of the shaft designed to be held by the player and any material added to it for the purpose of obtaining a firm hold. The grip shall be substantially straight and plain in form and shall not be molded for any part of the hands.

d. Clubhead
The distance from the heel to the toe of the clubhead shall be greater than the distance from the face to the back. The clubhead shall be generally plain in shape.

The clubhead shall have only one face designed for striking the ball, except that a putter may have two such faces if their characteristics are the same, they are opposite each other and the loft of each is the same and does not exceed 10 degrees.

e. Club Face
The face shall not have any degree of concavity and, in relation to the ball, shall be hard and rigid. It shall be generally smooth except for such markings as are permitted by Appendix II.

f. Wear
A club which conforms with Rule 4-1 when new is deemed to conform after wear through normal use. Any part of a club which has been purposely altered is regarded as new and must conform, in the altered state, with the Rules.

g. Damage
If a player's club ceases to conform with **Rule 4-1** because of damage sustained in the normal course of play, the player may:

(i) use the club in its damaged state, but only for the remainder of the <u>stipulated round</u> during which such damage was sustained; or

(ii) without unduly delaying play, repair it.

A club which ceases to conform because of damage sustained other than in the normal course of play shall not subsequently be used during the round.

(Damage changing playing characteristics of club — see Rule 4-2.)

(Damage rendering club unfit for play — see Rule 4-4a.)

4-2. Playing Characteristics Changed
During a <u>stipulated round</u>, the playing characteristics of a club shall not be purposely changed by adjustment or by any other means.

If the playing characteristics of a player's club are changed during a round because of damage sustained in the normal course of play, the player may:

(i) use the club in its altered state; or

(ii) without unduly delaying play, repair it.

If the playing characteristics of a player's club are changed because of damage sustained other than in the normal course of play, the club shall not subsequently be used during the round.

Damage to a club which occurred prior to a round may be repaired during the round, provided the playing characteristics are not changed and play is not unduly delayed.

4-3. Foreign Material
No foreign material shall be applied to the club face for the purpose of influencing the movement of the ball.

Penalty for Breach of Rule 4-1, -2 or -3:
Disqualification.

4-4. Maximum of Fourteen Clubs

a. Selection and Replacement of Clubs
The player shall start a <u>stipulated round</u> with not more than fourteen clubs. He is limited to the clubs thus selected for that round except that, without unduly delaying play, he may:

(i) if he started with fewer than fourteen, add as many as will bring his total to that number; and

(ii) replace, with any club, a club which becomes unfit for play in the normal course of play.

The addition or replacement of a club or clubs may not be made by borrowing any club selected for play by any other person playing on the course.

b. Partners May Share Clubs
Partners may share clubs, provided that the total number of clubs carried by the partners so sharing does not exceed fourteen.

Penalty for Breach of Rule 4-4a or b,
Regardless of Number of Excess Clubs Carried:

Match play — At the conclusion of the hole at which the breach is discovered, the state of the match shall be adjusted by deducting one hole for each hole at which a breach occurred. Maximum deduction per round: two holes.

Stroke play — Two strokes for each hole at which any breach occurred; maximum penalty per round: four strokes.

Bogey and par competitions — Penalties as in match play.

Stableford competitions — See Note to Rule 32-1b.

c. Excess Club Declared Out of Play
Any club carried or used in breach of this Rule shall be declared out of play by the player immediately upon discovery that a breach has occurred and thereafter shall not be used by the player during the round.

Penalty for Breach of Rule 4-4c: *Disqualification.*

Rule 5. The Ball

5-1. General
The ball the player uses shall conform to specifications set forth in Appendix III on maximum weight, minimum size, spherical symmetry, initial velocity and overall distance when tested under specified conditions.

5-2. Foreign Material
No foreign material shall be applied to a ball for the purpose of changing its playing characteristics.

Penalty for Breach of Rule 5-1 or 5-2: *Disqualification.*

5-3. Ball Unfit for Play
A ball is unfit for play if it is visibly cut, cracked or out of shape. A ball is not unfit for play solely because mud or other materials adhere to it, its surface is scratched or scraped or its paint is damaged or discolored.

If a player has reason to believe his ball has become unfit for play during the play of the hole being played, he may during the play of such hole lift his ball without penalty to determine whether it is unfit.

Before lifting the ball, the player must announce his intention to his opponent in match play or his marker or a fellow-competitor in stroke play and mark the position of the ball. He may then lift and examine the ball without cleaning it and must give his opponent, marker or fellow-competitor an opportunity to examine the ball.

If he fails to comply with this procedure, *he shall incur a penalty of one stroke.*

If it is determined that the ball has become unfit for play during play of the hole being played, the player may substitute another ball, placing it on the spot where the original ball lay. Otherwise, the original ball shall be replaced.

If a ball breaks into pieces as a result of a stroke, the stroke shall be cancelled and the player shall play a ball without penalty as nearly as possible at the spot from which the original ball was played (see Rule 20-5).

*PENALTY FOR BREACH OF RULE 5-3:
Match play — Loss of hole; Stroke play — Two strokes.

If a player incurs the general penalty for breach of Rule 5-3, no additional penalty under the Rule shall be applied.

Note: If the opponent, marker or fellow-competitor wishes to dispute a claim of unfitness, he must do so before the player plays another ball.

(Cleaning ball lifted from putting green or under any other Rule — see Rule 21.)

PLAYER'S RESPONSIBILITIES
Rule 6. The Player

Definition

A "marker" is one who is appointed by the Committee to record a competitor's score in stroke play. He may be a fellow-competitor. He is not a referee.

6-1. Conditions of Competition

The player is responsible for knowing the conditions under which the competition is to be played (Rule 33-1).

6-2. Handicap

a. MATCH PLAY

Before starting a match in a handicap competition, the players should determine from one another their respective handicaps. If a player begins the match having declared a higher handicap which would affect the number of strokes given or received, *he shall be disqualified*; otherwise, the player shall play off the declared handicap.

b. STROKE PLAY

In any round of a handicap competition, the competitor shall ensure that his handicap is recorded on his score card before it is returned to the Committee. If no handicap is recorded on his score card before it is returned, or if the recorded handicap is higher than that to which he is entitled and this affects the number of strokes received, *he shall be disqualified* from that round of the handicap competition; otherwise, the score shall stand.

Note: It is the player's responsibility to know the holes at which handicap strokes are to be given or received.

6-3. Time of Starting and Groups

a. TIME OF STARTING

The player shall start at the time laid down by the Committee.

b. GROUPS

In stroke play, the competitor shall remain throughout the round in the group arranged by the Committee unless the Committee authorizes or ratifies a change.

PENALTY FOR BREACH OF RULE 6-3: *Disqualification.*

(Best-ball and four-ball play — see Rules 30-3a and 31-2.)

Note: The Committee may provide in the conditions of a competition (Rule 33-1) that, if the player arrives at his starting point, ready to play, within five minutes after his starting time, in the absence of circumstances which warrant waiving the penalty of disqualification as provided in Rule 33-7, the penalty for failure to start on time is *loss of the first hole in match play or two strokes at the first hole in stroke play* instead of disqualification.

6-4. Caddie

The player may have only one caddie at any one time, *under penalty of disqualification.*

For any breach of a Rule by his caddie, the player incurs the applicable penalty.

6-5. Ball

The responsibility for playing the proper ball rests with the player. Each player should put an identification mark on his ball.

6-6. Scoring in Stroke Play

a. RECORDING SCORES

After each hole the marker should check the score with the competitor and record it. On completion of the round the marker shall sign the card and hand it to the competitor. If more than one marker records the scores, each shall sign for the part for which he is responsible.

b. SIGNING AND RETURNING CARD

After completion of the round, the competitor should check his score for each hole and settle any doubtful points with the Committee. He shall ensure that the marker has signed the card, countersign the card himself and return it to the Committee as soon as possible.

PENALTY FOR BREACH OF RULE 6-6b: *Disqualification.*

c. ALTERATION OF CARD

No alteration may be made on a card after the competitor has returned it to the Committee.

d. WRONG SCORE FOR HOLE

The competitor is responsible for the correctness of the score recorded for each hole. If he returns a score for any hole lower than actually taken, *he shall be disqualified*. If he returns a score for any hole higher than actually taken, the score as returned shall stand.

Note 1: The Committee is responsible for the addition of scores and application of the handicap recorded on the card — see Rule 33-5.

Note 2: In four-ball stroke play, see also Rule 31-4 and -7a.

6-7. Undue Delay

The player shall play without undue delay. Between completion of a hole and playing from the next teeing ground, the player shall not unduly delay play.

PENALTY FOR BREACH OF RULE 6-7:
*Match play — Loss of hole; Stroke play — Two strokes. For repeated offense — Disqualification.
If the player unduly delays play between holes, he is delaying the play of the next hole and the penalty applies to that hole.*

6-8. Discontinuance of Play

a. WHEN PERMITTED

The player shall not discontinue play unless:
    (i) the Committee has suspended play;
    (ii) he believes there is danger from lightning;
    (iii) he is seeking a decision from the Committee on a doubtful or disputed point (see Rules 2-5 and 34-3); or
    (iv) there is some other good reason such as sudden illness.

Bad weather is not of itself a good reason for discontinuing play.

If the player discontinues play without specific permission from the Committee, he shall report to the Committee as soon as practicable. If he does so and the Committee considers his reason satisfactory, the player incurs no penalty. Otherwise, *the player shall be disqualified.*

Exception in match play: Players discontinuing match play by agreement are not subject to disqualification unless by so doing the competition is delayed.

Note: Leaving the course does not of itself constitute discontinuance of play.

b. PROCEDURE WHEN PLAY SUSPENDED BY COMMITTEE

When play is suspended by the Committee, if the players in a match or group are between the play of two holes, they shall not resume play until the Committee has ordered a resumption of play. If they are in the process of playing a hole, they may continue provided they do so without delay. If they choose to continue, they shall discontinue either before or immediately after completing the hole, and shall not thereafter resume play until the Committee has ordered a resumption of play.

When play has been suspended by the Committee, the player shall resume play when the Committee has ordered a resumption of play.

PENALTY FOR BREACH OF RULE 6-8b: *Disqualification.*

c. LIFTING BALL WHEN PLAY DISCONTINUED

When during the play of a hole a player discontinues play under Rule 6-8a, he may lift his ball. A ball may be cleaned when so lifted. If a ball has been so lifted, the player shall, when play is resumed, place a ball on the spot from which the original ball was lifted.

PENALTY FOR BREACH OF RULE 6-8c:
Match play — Loss of hole; Stroke play — Two strokes.

Rule 7. Practice

7-1. Before or Between Rounds

a. MATCH PLAY

On any day of a match play competition, a player may practice on the competition course before a round.

b. STROKE PLAY

On any day of a stroke competition or play-off, a competitor shall not practice on the competition course or test the surface of any putting green on the course before a round or play-off. When two or more rounds of a stroke competition are to be played over consecutive days, practice between those rounds on any competition course remaining to be played is prohibited.

Exception: Practice putting or chipping on or near the first teeing ground before starting a round or play-off is permitted.

PENALTY FOR BREACH OF RULE 7-1b: *Disqualification.*

Note: The Committee may in the conditions of a competition (Rule 33-1) prohibit practice on the competition course on any day of a match play competition or permit practice on the competition course or part of the course (Rule 33-2c) on any day of or between rounds of a stroke competition.

7-2. During Round

A player shall not play a practice stroke either during the play of a hole or between the play of two holes except that, between the play of two holes, the player may practice putting or chipping on or near the putting green of the hole last played, any practice putting green or the teeing ground of the next hole to be played in the round, provided such practice stroke is not played from a hazard and does not unduly delay play (Rule 6-7).

Exception: When play has been suspended by the Committee, a player may, prior to resumption of play, practice (a) as provided in this Rule, (b) anywhere other than on the competition course and (c) as otherwise permitted by the Committee.

PENALTY FOR BREACH OF RULE 7-2:
Match play — Loss of hole; Stroke play — Two strokes.
In the event of a breach between the play of two holes, the penalty applies to the next hole.

Note 1: A practice swing is not a practice stroke and may be taken at any place, provided the player does not breach the Rules.

Note 2: The Committee may prohibit practice on or near the putting green of the hole last played.

Rule 8. Advice; Indicating Line of Play

Definitions

"Advice" is any counsel or suggestion which could influence a player in determining his play, the choice of a club or the method of making a stroke.

Information on the Rules or on matters of public information, such as the position of hazards or the flagstick on the putting green, is not advice.

The "line of play" is the direction which the player wishes his ball to take after a stroke, plus a reasonable distance on either side of the intended direction. The line of play extends vertically upwards from the ground, but does not extend beyond the hole.

8-1. Advice

A player shall not give advice to anyone in the competition except his partner. A player may ask for advice from only his partner or either of their caddies.

8-2. Indicating Line of Play

a. OTHER THAN ON PUTTING GREEN

Except on the putting green, a player may have the line of play indicated to him by anyone, but no one shall stand on or close to the line while the stroke is being played. Any mark placed during the play of a hole by the player or with his knowledge to indicate the line shall be removed before the stroke is played.

Exception: Flagstick attended or held up — see Rule 17-1.

b. ON THE PUTTING GREEN

When the player's ball is on the putting green, the player, his partner or either of their caddies may, before but not during the stroke, point out a line for putting, but in so doing the putting green shall not be touched. No mark shall be placed anywhere to indicate a line for putting.

PENALTY FOR BREACH OF RULE:
Match play — Loss of hole; Stroke play — Two strokes.

Note: In a team competition with or without concurrent individual competition, the Committee may in the conditions of the competition (Rule 33-1) permit each team to appoint one person, *e.g.*, team captain or coach, who may give advice (including pointing out a line for putting) to members of that team. Such person shall be identified to the Committee prior to the start of the competition.

Rule 9. Information as to Strokes Taken

9-1. General

The number of strokes a player has taken shall include any penalty strokes incurred.

9-2. Match Play

A player who has incurred a penalty shall inform his opponent as soon as practicable, unless he is obviously proceeding under a Rule involving a penalty and this has been observed by his opponent. If he fails so to inform his opponent, he shall be deemed to have given wrong information, even if he was not aware that he had incurred a penalty.

An opponent is entitled to ascertain from the player, during the play of a hole, the number of strokes he has taken and, after play of a hole, the number of strokes taken on the hole just completed.

If during the play of a hole the player gives or is deemed to give wrong information as to the number of strokes taken, he shall incur no penalty if he corrects the mistake before his opponent has played his next stroke. If the player fails so to correct the wrong information, *he shall lose the hole.*

If after play of a hole the player gives or is deemed to give wrong information as to the number of strokes taken on the hole just completed and this affects the opponent's understanding of the result of the hole, he shall incur no penalty if he corrects his mistake before any player plays from the next <u>teeing ground</u> or, in the case of the last hole of the match, before all players leave the <u>putting green</u>. If the player fails so to correct the wrong information, *he shall lose the hole.*

9-3. Stroke Play

A competitor who has incurred a penalty should inform his marker as soon as practicable.

ORDER OF PLAY
Rule 10. Order of Play

10-1. Match Play

a. TEEING GROUND

The side entitled to play first from the <u>teeing ground</u> is said to have the "honor."

The side which shall have the honor at the first teeing ground shall be determined by the order of the draw. In the absence of a draw, the honor should be decided by lot.

The side which wins a hole shall take the honor at the next teeing ground. If a hole has been halved, the side which had the honor at the previous teeing ground shall retain it.

b. OTHER THAN ON TEEING GROUND

When the balls are in play, the ball farther from the hole shall be played first. If the balls are equidistant from the hole, the ball to be played first should be decided by lot.

Exception: Rule 30-3c (best-ball and four-ball match play).

c. PLAYING OUT OF TURN

If a player plays when his opponent should have played, the opponent may immediately require the player to cancel the stroke so played and, in correct order, play a ball without penalty as nearly as possible at the spot from which the original ball was last played (see Rule 20-5).

10-2. Stroke Play

a. TEEING GROUND

The competitor entitled to play first from the <u>teeing ground</u> is said to have the "honor."

The competitor who shall have the honor at the first teeing ground shall be determined by the order of the draw. In the absence of a draw, the honor should be decided by lot.

The competitor with the lowest score at a hole shall take the honor at the next teeing ground. The competitor with the second lowest score shall play next and so on. If two or more competitors have the same score at a hole, they shall play from the next teeing ground in the same order as at the previous teeing ground.

b. OTHER THAN ON TEEING GROUND

When the balls are in play, the ball farthest from the hole shall be played first. If two or more balls are equidistant from the hole, the ball to be played first should be decided by lot.

Exceptions: Rules 22 (ball interfering with or assisting play) and 31-5 (four-ball stroke play).

c. PLAYING OUT OF TURN

If a competitor plays out of turn, no penalty is incurred and the ball shall be played as it lies. If, however, the Committee determines that competitors have agreed to play in an order other than that set forth in Clauses 2a and 2b of this Rule to give one of them an advantage, *they shall be disqualified.*

(Incorrect order of play in threesomes and foursomes stroke play — see Rule 29-3.)

10-3. Provisional Ball or Second Ball from Teeing Ground

If a player plays a <u>provisional ball</u> or a second ball from a <u>teeing ground</u>, he should do so after his opponent or fellow-competitor has played his first <u>stroke</u>. If a player plays a provisional ball or a second ball out of turn, Clauses 1c and 2c of this Rule shall apply.

10-4. Ball Moved in Measuring

If a ball is moved in measuring to determine which ball is farther from the hole, no penalty is incurred and the ball shall be replaced.

TEEING GROUND
Rule 11. Teeing Ground

Definition

The "teeing ground" is the starting place for the hole to be played. It is a rectangular area two club-lengths in depth, the front and the sides of which are defined by the outside limits of two tee-markers. A ball is outside the teeing ground when all of it lies outside the teeing ground.

11-1. Teeing

In teeing, the ball may be placed on the ground, on an irregularity of surface created by the player on the ground or on a tee, sand or other substance in order to raise it off the ground.

A player may stand outside the <u>teeing ground</u> to play a ball within it.

11-2. Tee-Markers

Before a player plays his first stroke with any ball from the teeing ground of the hole being played, the tee-markers are deemed to be fixed. In such circumstances, if the player moves or allows to be moved a tee-marker for the purpose of avoiding interference with his stance, the area of his intended swing or his line of play, *he shall incur the penalty for a breach of Rule 13-2.*

11-3. Ball Falling Off Tee

If a ball, when not <u>in play</u>, falls off a tee or is knocked off a tee by the player in addressing it, it may be re-teed without penalty, but if a <u>stroke</u> is made at the ball in these circumstances, whether the ball is moving or not, the stroke counts but no penalty is incurred.

11-4. Playing from Outside Teeing Ground

a. MATCH PLAY

If a player, when starting a hole, plays a ball from outside the <u>teeing ground</u>, the opponent may immediately require the player to cancel the stroke so played and play a ball from within the teeing ground, without penalty.

b. STROKE PLAY

If a competitor, when starting a hole, plays a ball from outside the <u>teeing ground</u>, *he shall incur a penalty of two strokes* and shall then play a ball from within the teeing ground.

If the competitor plays a stroke from the next teeing ground without first correcting his mistake or, in the case of the last hole of the round, leaves the <u>putting green</u> without first declaring his intention to correct his mistake, *he shall be disqualified.*

Strokes played by a competitor from outside the teeing ground do not count in his score.

11-5. Playing from Wrong Teeing Ground

The provisions of Rule 11-4 apply.

PLAYING THE BALL

Rule 12. Searching for and Identifying Ball

Definitions

A "hazard" is any <u>bunker</u> or <u>water hazard</u>.

A "bunker" is a <u>hazard</u> consisting of a prepared area of ground, often a hollow, from which turf or soil has been removed and replaced with sand or the like. Grass-covered ground bordering or within a bunker is not part of the bunker. The margin of a bunker extends vertically downwards, but not upwards.

A "water hazard" is any sea, lake, pond, river, ditch, surface drainage ditch or other open water course (whether or not containing water) and anything of a similar nature.

All ground or water within the margin of a water hazard is part of the water hazard. The margin of a water hazard extends vertically upwards and downwards. Stakes and lines defining the margins of water hazards are in the hazards.

12-1. Searching for Ball; Seeing Ball

In searching for his ball anywhere on the course, the player may touch or bend long grass, rushes, bushes, whins, heather or the like, but only to the extent necessary to find and identify it, provided that this does not improve the lie of the ball, the area of his intended swing or his line of play.

A player is not necessarily entitled to see his ball when playing a stroke.

In a <u>hazard</u>, if a ball is covered by <u>loose impediments</u> or sand, the player may remove by probing, raking or other means as much thereof as will enable him to see a part of the ball. If an excess is removed, no penalty is incurred and the ball shall be re-covered so that only a part of the ball is visible. If the ball is moved in such removal, no penalty is incurred; the ball shall be replaced and, if necessary, re-covered. As to removal of loose impediments outside a hazard, see Rule 23.

If a ball lying in <u>casual water,</u> <u>ground under repair</u> or a hole, cast or runway made by a burrowing animal, a reptile or a bird is accidentally moved during search, no penalty is incurred; the ball shall be replaced, unless the player elects to proceed under Rule 25-1b.

If a ball is believed to be lying in water in a <u>water hazard</u>, the player may probe for it with a club or otherwise. If the ball is moved in so doing, no penalty is incurred; the ball shall be replaced, unless the player elects to proceed under Rule 26-1.

PENALTY FOR BREACH OF RULE 12-1:
Match play — Loss of hole; Stroke play — Two strokes.

12-2. Identifying Ball

The responsibility for playing the proper ball rests with the player. Each player should put an identification mark on his ball.

Except in a <u>hazard</u>, the player may, without penalty, lift a ball he believes to be his own for the purpose of identification and clean it to the extent necessary for identification. If the ball is the player's ball, he shall replace it. Before lifting the ball, the player must announce his intention to his opponent in match play or his marker or a fellow-competitor in stroke play and mark the position of the ball. He must then give his opponent, marker or fellow-competitor an opportunity to observe the lifting and replacement. If he lifts his ball without announcing his intention in advance, marking the position of the ball or giving his opponent, marker or fellow-competitor an opportunity to observe, or if he lifts his ball for identification in a hazard, or cleans it more than necessary for identification, *he shall incur a penalty of one stroke* and the ball shall be replaced.

If a player who is required to replace a ball fails to do so, *he shall incur the penalty* for a breach of Rule 20-3a, but no additional penalty under Rule 12-2 shall be applied.

Rule 13. Ball Played as It Lies; Lie, Area of Intended Swing and Line of Play; Stance

Definitions

A "hazard" is any <u>bunker</u> or <u>water hazard</u>.

A "bunker" is a <u>hazard</u> consisting of a prepared area of ground, often a hollow, from which turf or soil has been removed and replaced with sand or the like. Grass-covered ground bordering or within a bunker is not part of the bunker. The margin of a bunker extends vertically downwards, but not upwards.

A "water hazard" is any sea, lake, pond, river, ditch, surface drainage ditch or other open water course (whether or not containing water) and anything of a similar nature.

All ground or water within the margin of a water hazard is part of the water hazard. The margin of a water hazard extends vertically upwards and downwards. Stakes and lines defining the margins of water hazards are in the hazards.

The "line of play" is the direction which the player wishes his ball to take after a stroke, plus a reasonable distance on either side of the intended direction. The line of play extends vertically upwards from the ground, but does not extend beyond the hole.

13-1. Ball Played as It Lies

The ball shall be played as it lies, except as otherwise provided in the Rules.

(Ball at rest moved — see Rule 18.)

13-2. Improving Lie, Area of Intended Swing or Line of Play

Except as provided in the Rules, a player shall not improve or allow to be improved:

the position or lie of his ball,

the area of his intended swing,

his <u>line of play</u> or

a reasonable extension of that line beyond the hole or the area in which he is to drop or place a ball

by any of the following actions:

moving, bending or breaking anything growing or fixed (including immovable <u>obstructions</u> and objects defining <u>out of bounds</u>) or

removing or pressing down sand, loose soil, replaced divots, other cut turf placed in position or other irregularities of surface

except as follows:

as may occur in fairly taking his <u>stance</u>,

in making a <u>stroke</u> or the backward movement of his club for a stroke,

on the <u>teeing ground</u> in creating or eliminating irregularities of surface, or

on the <u>putting green</u> in removing sand and loose soil as provided in Rule 16-1a or in repairing damage as provided in Rule 16-1c.

The club may be grounded only lightly and shall not be pressed on the ground.

Exception: Ball lying in or touching hazard — see Rule 13-4.

13-3. Building Stance

A player is entitled to place his feet firmly in taking his stance, but he shall not build a stance.

13-4. Ball Lying in or Touching Hazard

Except as provided in the Rules, before making a <u>stroke</u> at a ball which lies in or touches a <u>hazard</u> (whether a <u>bunker</u> or a <u>water hazard</u>), the player shall not:

a. Test the condition of the hazard or any similar hazard,

b. Touch the ground in the hazard or water in the water hazard with a club or otherwise, or

c. Touch or move a loose impediment lying in or touching the hazard.

Exceptions:

1. Provided nothing is done which constitutes testing the condition of the hazard or improves the lie of the ball, there is no penalty if the player (a) touches the ground in any hazard or water in a water hazard as a result of or to prevent falling, in removing an obstruction, in measuring or in retrieving or lifting a ball under any Rule or (b) places his clubs in a hazard.

2. The player after playing the stroke, or his caddie at any time without the authority of the player, may smooth sand or soil in the hazard, provided that, if the ball still lies in the hazard, nothing is done which improves the lie of the ball or assists the player in his subsequent play of the hole.

Note: At any time, including at address or in the backward movement for the stroke, the player may touch with a club or otherwise any obstruction, any construction declared by the Committee to be an integral part of the course or any grass, bush, tree or other growing thing.

PENALTY FOR BREACH OF RULE:
Match play — Loss of hole; Stroke play — Two strokes.

(Searching for ball — see Rule 12-1.)

Rule 14. Striking the Ball

Definition

A "stroke" is the forward movement of the club made with the intention of fairly striking at and moving the ball, but if a player checks his downswing voluntarily before the clubhead reaches the ball he is deemed not to have made a stroke.

14-1. Ball to Be Fairly Struck At

The ball shall be fairly struck at with the head of the club and must not be pushed, scraped or spooned.

14-2. Assistance

In making a stroke, a player shall not accept physical assistance or protection from the elements.

PENALTY FOR BREACH OF RULE 14-1 OR -2:
Match play — Loss of hole; Stroke play — Two strokes.

14-3. Artificial Devices and Unusual Equipment

If there may be any reasonable basis for doubt as to whether an item which is to be manufactured would, if used by a player during a round, cause the player to be in breach of Rule 14-3, the manufacturer should submit a sample to the United States Golf Association for a ruling, such sample to become its property for reference purposes. If a manufacturer fails to do so, he assumes the risk of an unfavorable ruling.

A player in doubt as to whether use of an item would constitute a breach of Rule 14-3 should consult the United States Golf Association.

Except as provided in the Rules, during a stipulated round the player shall not use any artificial device or unusual equipment:

a. Which might assist him in making a stroke or in his play; or

b. For the purpose of gauging or measuring distance or conditions which might affect his play; or

c. Which might assist him in gripping the club, except that plain gloves may be worn, resin, tape or gauze may be applied to the grip (provided such application does not render the grip non-conforming under Rule 4-1c) and a towel or handkerchief may be wrapped around the grip.

PENALTY FOR BREACH OF RULE 14-3: *Disqualification.*

14-4. Striking the Ball More than Once

If a player's club strikes the ball more than once in the course of a stroke, the player shall count the stroke and *add a penalty stroke,* making two strokes in all.

14-5. Playing Moving Ball

A player shall not play while his ball is moving.

Exceptions:
Ball falling off tee — Rule 11-3.
Striking the ball more than once — Rule 14-4.
Ball moving in water — Rule 14-6.

When the ball begins to move only after the player has begun the stroke or the backward movement of his club for the stroke, he shall incur no penalty under this Rule for playing a moving ball, but he is not exempt from any penalty incurred under the following Rules:
Ball at rest moved by player — Rule 18-2a.
Ball at rest moving after address — Rule 18-2b.
Ball at rest moving after loose impediment touched — Rule 18-2c.

14-6. Ball Moving in Water

When a ball is moving in water in a water hazard, the player may, without penalty, make a stroke, but he must not delay making his stroke in order to allow the wind or current to improve the position of the ball. A ball moving in water in a water hazard may be lifted if the player elects to invoke Rule 26.

PENALTY FOR BREACH OF RULE 14-5 OR -6:
Match play — Loss of hole; Stroke play — Two strokes.

Rule 15. Playing a Wrong Ball

Definition

A "wrong ball" is any ball other than:
a. The ball in play,
b. A provisional ball or
c. In stroke play, a second ball played under Rule 3-3 or Rule 20-7b.

Note: Ball in play includes a ball substituted for the ball in play when the player is proceeding under an applicable Rule which does not permit substitution.

15-1. General

A player must hole out with the ball played from the teeing ground unless a Rule permits him to substitute another ball. If a player substitutes another ball when proceeding under an applicable Rule which does not permit substitution, that ball is not a wrong ball; it becomes the ball in play and, if the error is not corrected as provided in Rule 20-6, *the player shall incur a penalty of loss of hole in match play or two strokes in stroke play.*

15-2. Match Play

If a player plays a stroke with a wrong ball except in a hazard, *he shall lose the hole.*

If a player plays any strokes in a hazard with a wrong ball, there is no penalty. Strokes played in a hazard with a wrong ball do not count in the player's score. If the wrong ball belongs to another player, its owner shall place a ball on the spot from which the wrong ball was first played.

If the player and opponent exchange balls during the play of a hole, the first to play the wrong ball other than from a hazard shall lose the hole; when this cannot be determined, the hole shall be played out with the balls exchanged.

15-3. Stroke Play

If a competitor plays a stroke or strokes with a wrong ball, *he shall incur a penalty of two strokes,* unless the only stroke or strokes played with such ball were played when it was lying in a hazard, in which case no penalty is incurred.

The competitor must correct his mistake by playing the correct ball. If he fails to correct his mistake before he plays a stroke from the next teeing ground or, in the case of the last hole of the round, fails to declare his intention to correct his mistake before leaving the putting green, *he shall be disqualified.*

Strokes played by a competitor with a wrong ball do not count in his score.

If the wrong ball belongs to another competitor, its owner shall place a ball on the spot from which the wrong ball was first played.

(Lie of ball to be placed or replaced altered — see Rule 20-3b.)

THE PUTTING GREEN

Rule 16. The Putting Green

Definitions

The "putting green" is all ground of the hole being played which is specially prepared for putting or otherwise defined as such by the Committee. A ball is on the putting green when any part of it touches the putting green.

The "line of putt" is the line which the player wishes his ball to take after a stroke on the putting green. Except with respect to Rule 16-1e, the line of putt includes a reasonable distance on either side of the intended line. The line of putt does not extend beyond the hole.

A ball is "holed" when it is at rest within the circumference of the hole and all of it is below the level of the lip of the hole.

16-1. General

a. TOUCHING LINE OF PUTT

The line of putt must not be touched except:

(i) the player may move sand and loose soil on the putting green and other loose impediments by picking them up or by brushing them aside with his hand or a club without pressing anything down;

(ii) in addressing the ball, the player may place the club in front of the ball without pressing anything down;

(iii) in measuring — Rule 10-4;

(iv) in lifting the ball — Rule 16-1b;

(v) in pressing down a ball-marker;

(vi) in repairing old hole plugs or ball marks on the putting green — Rule 16-1c; and

(vii) in removing movable obstructions — Rule 24-1.

(Indicating line for putting on putting green — see Rule 8-2b.)

b. LIFTING BALL

A ball on the putting green may be lifted and, if desired, cleaned. A ball so lifted shall be replaced on the spot from which it was lifted.

c. REPAIR OF HOLE PLUGS, BALL MARKS AND OTHER DAMAGE

The player may repair an old hole plug or damage to the putting green caused by the impact of a ball, whether or not the player's ball lies on the putting green. If the ball is moved in the process of such repair, it shall be replaced, without penalty. Any other damage to the putting green shall not be repaired if it might assist the player in his subsequent play of the hole.

d. TESTING SURFACE

During the play of a hole, a player shall not test the surface of the putting green by rolling a ball or roughening or scraping the surface.

e. STANDING ASTRIDE OR ON LINE OF PUTT

The player shall not make a stroke on the putting green from a stance astride, or with either foot touching, the line of putt or an extension of that line behind the ball.

f. POSITION OF CADDIE OR PARTNER

While making a stroke on the putting green, the player shall not allow his caddie, his partner or his partner's caddie to position himself on or close to an extension of the line of putt behind the ball.

g. PLAYING STROKE WHILE ANOTHER BALL IN MOTION

The player shall not play a stroke while another ball is in motion after a stroke from the putting green, except that, if a player does so, he incurs no penalty if it was his turn to play.

(Lifting ball interfering with or assisting play while another ball in motion — see Rule 22.)

PENALTY FOR BREACH OF RULE 16-1:
Match play — Loss of hole; Stroke play — Two strokes.

16-2. Ball Overhanging Hole

When any part of the ball overhangs the lip of the hole, the player is allowed enough time to reach the hole without unreasonable delay and an additional ten seconds to determine whether the ball is at rest. If by then the ball has not fallen into the hole, it is deemed to be at rest. If the ball subsequently falls into the hole, the player is deemed to have holed out with his last stroke, and *he shall add a penalty stroke to his score* for the hole; otherwise there is no penalty under this Rule.

(Undue delay — see Rule 6-7.)

Rule 17. The Flagstick

17-1. Flagstick Attended, Removed or Held Up

Before and during the stroke, the player may have the flagstick attended, removed or held up to indicate the position of the hole. This may be done only on the authority of the player before he plays his stroke.

If, prior to the stroke, the flagstick is attended, removed or held up by anyone with the player's knowledge and no objection is made, the player shall be deemed to have authorized it. If anyone attends or holds up the flagstick or stands near the hole while a stroke is being played, he shall be deemed to be attending the flagstick until the ball comes to rest.

17-2. Unauthorized Attendance

a. MATCH PLAY

In match play, an opponent or his caddie shall not, without the authority or prior knowledge of the player, attend, remove or hold up the flagstick while the player is making a stroke or his ball is in motion.

b. STROKE PLAY

In stroke play, if a fellow-competitor or his caddie attends, removes or holds up the flagstick without the competitor's authority or prior knowledge while the competitor is making a stroke or his ball is in motion, *the fellow-competitor shall incur the penalty* for breach of this Rule. In such circumstances, if the competitor's ball strikes the flagstick, the person attending it or anything carried by him, the competitor incurs no penalty and the ball shall be played as it lies, except that, if the stroke was played from the putting green, the stroke shall be cancelled, the ball replaced and the stroke replayed.

PENALTY FOR BREACH OF RULE 17-1 or -2:
Match play — Loss of hole; Stroke play — Two strokes.

17-3. Ball Striking Flagstick or Attendant

The player's ball shall not strike:

a. The flagstick when attended, removed or held up by the player, his partner or either of their caddies, or by another person with the player's authority or prior knowledge; or

b. The player's caddie, his partner or his partner's caddie when attending the flagstick, or another person attending the flagstick with the player's authority or prior knowledge or anything carried by any such person; or

c. The flagstick in the hole, unattended, when the ball has been played from the putting green.

PENALTY FOR BREACH OF RULE 17-3:
Match play — Loss of hole; Stroke play — Two strokes, and the ball shall be played as it lies.

17-4. Ball Resting Against Flagstick

If the ball rests against the flagstick when it is in the hole, the player or another person authorized by him may move or remove the flagstick and if the ball falls into the hole, the player shall be deemed to have holed out with his last stroke; otherwise, the ball, if moved, shall be placed on the lip of the hole, without penalty.

BALL MOVED, DEFLECTED OR STOPPED
Rule 18. Ball at Rest Moved

A ball is deemed to have "moved" if it leaves its position and comes to rest in any other place.

An "outside agency" is any agency not part of the match or, in stroke play, not part of the competitor's side, and includes a referee, a marker, an observer or a fore-caddie. Neither wind nor water is an outside agency.

"Equipment" is anything used, worn or carried by or for the player except any ball he has played at the hole being played and any small object, such as a coin or a tee, when used to mark the position of a ball or the extent of an area in which a ball is to be dropped. Equipment includes a golf cart, whether or not motorized. If such a cart is shared by two or more players, the cart and everything in it are deemed to be the equipment of the player whose ball is involved except that, when the cart is being moved by one of the players sharing it, the cart and everything in it are deemed to be that player's equipment.

Note: A ball played at the hole being played is equipment when it has been lifted and not put back into play.

A player has "addressed the ball" when he has taken his stance and has also grounded his club, except that in a hazard a player has addressed the ball when he has taken his stance.

Taking the "stance" consists in a player placing his feet in position for and preparatory to making a stroke.

18-1. By Outside Agency

If a ball at rest is moved by an outside agency, the player shall incur no penalty and the ball shall be replaced before the player plays another stroke.

(Player's ball at rest moved by another ball — see Rule 18-5.)

18-2. By Player, Partner, Caddie or Equipment
a. GENERAL

When a player's ball is in play, if:
(i) the player, his partner or either of their caddies lifts or moves it, touches it purposely (except with a club in the act of addressing it) or causes it to move except as permitted by a Rule, or
(ii) equipment of the player or his partner causes the ball to move,
the player shall incur a penalty stroke. The ball shall be replaced unless the movement of the ball occurs after the player has begun his swing and he does not discontinue his swing.

Under the Rules no penalty is incurred if a player accidentally causes his ball to move in the following circumstances:

In measuring to determine which ball farther from hole — Rule 10-4

In searching for covered ball in hazard or for ball in casual water, ground under repair, etc. — Rule 12-1

In the process of repairing hole plug or ball mark — Rule 16-1c

In the process of removing loose impediment on putting green — Rule 18-2c

In the process of lifting ball under a Rule — Rule 20-1

In the process of placing or replacing ball under a Rule — Rule 20-3a

In complying with Rule 22 relating to lifting ball interfering with or assisting play

In removal of movable obstruction — Rule 24-1.

b. BALL MOVING AFTER ADDRESS

If a player's ball in play moves after he has addressed it (other than as a result of a stroke), the player shall be deemed to have moved the ball and *shall incur a penalty stroke.* The player shall replace the ball unless the movement of the ball occurs after he has begun his swing and he does not discontinue his swing.

c. BALL MOVING AFTER LOOSE IMPEDIMENT TOUCHED

Through the green, if the ball moves after any loose impediment lying within a club-length of it has been touched by the player, his partner or either of their caddies and before the player has addressed it, the player shall be deemed to have moved the ball and *shall incur a penalty stroke.* The player shall replace the ball unless the movement of the ball occurs after he has begun his swing and he does not discontinue his swing.

On the putting green, if the ball or the ball-marker moves in the process of removing any loose impediment, the ball or the ball-marker shall be replaced. There is no penalty provided the movement of the ball or the ball-marker is directly attributable to the removal of the loose impediment. Otherwise, *the player shall incur a penalty stroke* under Rule 18-2a or 20-1.

18-3. By Opponent, Caddie or Equipment in Match Play

a. DURING SEARCH

If, during search for a player's ball, it is moved by an opponent, his caddie or his equipment, no penalty is incurred and the player shall replace the ball.

b. OTHER THAN DURING SEARCH

If, other than during search for a ball, the ball is touched or moved by an opponent, his caddie or his equipment, except as otherwise provided in the Rules, *the opponent shall incur a penalty stroke.* The player shall replace the ball.

(Ball moved in measuring to determine which ball farther from the hole — see Rule 10-4.)
(Playing a wrong ball — see Rule 15-2.)
(Ball moved in complying with Rule 22 relating to lifting ball interfering with or assisting play.)

18-4. By Fellow-Competitor, Caddie or Equipment In Stroke Play

If a competitor's ball is moved by a fellow-competitor, his caddie or his equipment, no penalty is incurred. The competitor shall replace his ball.

(Playing a wrong ball — see Rule 15-3.)

18-5. By Another Ball

If a ball in play and at rest is moved by another ball in motion after a stroke, the moved ball shall be replaced.

*PENALTY FOR BREACH OF RULE:
Match play — Loss of hole; Stroke play — Two strokes.
If a player who is required to replace a ball fails to do so, he shall incur the general penalty for breach of Rule 18 but no additional penalty under Rule 18 shall be applied.

Note 1: If a ball to be replaced under this Rule is not immediately recoverable, another ball may be substituted.

Note 2: If it is impossible to determine the spot on which a ball is to be placed, see Rule 20-3c.

Rule 19. Ball in Motion Deflected or Stopped

Definitions

An "outside agency" is any agency not part of the match or, in stroke play, not part of the competitor's side, and includes a referee, a marker, an observer or a fore-caddie. Neither wind nor water is an outside agency.

"Equipment" is anything used, worn or carried by or for the player except any ball he has played at the hole being played and any small object, such as a coin or a tee, when used to mark the position of a ball or the extent of an area in which a ball is to be dropped. Equipment includes a golf cart, whether or not motorized. If such a cart is shared by two or more players, the cart and everything in it are deemed to be the equipment of the player whose ball is involved except that, when the cart is being moved by one of the players sharing it, the cart and everything in it are deemed to be that player's equipment.

Note: A ball played at the hole being played is equipment when it has been lifted and not put back into play.

19-1. By Outside Agency

If a ball in motion is accidentally deflected or stopped by any outside agency, it is a rub of the green, no penalty is incurred and the ball shall be played as it lies except:

a. If a ball in motion after a stroke other than on the putting green comes to rest in or on any moving or animate outside agency, the player shall, through the green or in a hazard, drop the ball, or on the putting green place the ball, as near as possible to the spot where the outside agency was when the ball came to rest in or on it, and

b. If a ball in motion after a stroke on the putting green is deflected or stopped by, or comes to rest in or on, any moving or animate outside agency except a worm or an insect, the stroke shall be cancelled, the ball replaced and the stroke replayed.

If the ball is not immediately recoverable, another ball may be substituted.

(Player's ball deflected or stopped by another ball — see Rule 19-5.)

Note: If the referee or the Committee determines that a player's ball has been purposely deflected or stopped by an outside agency, Rule 1-4 applies to the player. If the outside agency is a fellow-competitor or his caddie, Rule 1-2 applies to the fellow-competitor.

19-2. By Player, Partner, Caddie or Equipment

a. MATCH PLAY

If a player's ball is accidentally deflected or stopped by himself, his partner or either of their caddies or equipment, *he shall lose the hole.*

b. STROKE PLAY

If a competitor's ball is accidentally deflected or stopped by himself, his partner or either of their caddies or equipment, *the competitor shall incur a penalty of two strokes.* The ball shall be played as it lies, except when it comes to rest in or on the competitor's, his partner's or either of their caddies' clothes or equipment, in which case the competitor shall through the green or in a hazard drop the ball, or on the putting green place the ball, as near as possible to where the article was when the ball came to rest in or on it.

Exception: Dropped ball — see Rule 20-2a.

(Ball purposely deflected or stopped by player, partner or caddie — see Rule 1-2.)

19-3. By Opponent, Caddie or Equipment in Match Play

If a player's ball is accidentally deflected or stopped by an opponent, his caddie or his equipment, no penalty is incurred. The player may play the ball as it lies or, before another stroke is played by either side, cancel the stroke and play a ball without penalty as nearly as possible at the spot from which the original ball was last played (see Rule 20-5).

If the ball has come to rest in or on the opponent's or his caddie's clothes or equipment, the player may through the green or in a hazard drop the ball, or on the putting green place the ball, as near as possible to where the article was when the ball came to rest in or on it.

Exception: Ball striking person attending flagstick — see Rule 17-3b.

(Ball purposely deflected or stopped by opponent or caddie — see Rule 1-2.)

19-4. By Fellow-Competitor, Caddie or Equipment in Stroke Play

See Rule 19-1 regarding ball deflected by outside agency.

19-5. By Another Ball

If a player's ball in motion after a stroke is deflected or stopped by a ball at rest, the player shall play his ball as it lies. In stroke play, if both balls lay on the putting green prior to the stroke, *the player incurs a penalty of two strokes.* Otherwise, no penalty is incurred.

If a player's ball in motion after a stroke is deflected or stopped by another ball in motion, the player shall play his ball as it lies. There is no penalty unless the player was in breach of Rule 16-1g, in which case *he shall incur the penalty for breach of that Rule.*

Exception: Ball in motion after a stroke on the putting green deflected or stopped by moving or animate outside agency — see Rule 19-1b.

PENALTY FOR BREACH OF RULE:
Match play — Loss of hole; Stroke play — Two strokes.

RELIEF SITUATIONS AND PROCEDURE
Rule 20. Lifting, Dropping and Placing; Playing from Wrong Place

20-1. Lifting

A ball to be lifted under the Rules may be lifted by the player, his partner or another person authorized by the player. In any such case, the player shall be responsible for any breach of the Rules.

The position of the ball shall be marked before it is lifted under a Rule which requires it to be replaced. If it is not marked, *the player shall incur a penalty of one stroke* and the ball shall be replaced. If it is not replaced, *the player shall incur the general penalty* for breach of this Rule but no additional penalty under Rule 20-1 shall be applied.

If a ball or the ball-marker is accidentally moved in the process of lifting the ball under a Rule or marking its position, the ball or the ball-marker shall be replaced. There is no penalty provided the movement of the ball or the ball-marker is directly attributable to the specific act of marking the position of or lifting the ball. Otherwise, *the player shall incur a penalty stroke* under this Rule or Rule 18-2a.

Exception: If a player incurs a penalty for failing to act in accordance with Rule 5-3 or 12-2, no additional penalty under Rule 20-1 shall be applied.

Note: The position of a ball to be lifted should be marked by placing a ball-marker, a small coin or other similar object immediately behind the ball. If the ball-marker interferes with the play, stance or stroke of another player, it should be placed one or more clubhead-lengths to one side.

20-2. Dropping and Re-dropping

a. By Whom and How

A ball to be dropped under the Rules shall be dropped by the player himself. He shall stand erect, hold the ball at shoulder height and arm's length and drop it. If a ball is dropped by any other person or in any other manner and the error is not corrected as provided in Rule 20-6, *the player shall incur a penalty stroke.*

If the ball touches the player, his partner, either of their caddies or their equipment before or after it strikes a part of the course, the ball shall be re-dropped, without penalty. There is no limit to the number of times a ball shall be re-dropped in such circumstances.

(Taking action to influence position or movement of ball — see Rule 1-2.)

b. Where to Drop

When a ball is to be dropped as near as possible to a specific spot, it shall be dropped not nearer the hole than the specific spot which, if it is not precisely known to the player, shall be estimated.

A ball when dropped must first strike a part of the course where the applicable Rule requires it to be dropped. If it is not so dropped, Rules 20-6 and -7 apply.

c. When to Re-Drop

A dropped ball shall be re-dropped without penalty if it:

(i) rolls into a hazard;

(ii) rolls out of a hazard;

(iii) rolls onto a putting green;

(iv) rolls out of bounds;

(v) rolls to a position where there is interference by the condition from which relief was taken under Rule 24-2 (immovable obstruction) or Rule 25-1 (abnormal ground condition);

(vi) rolls and comes to rest more than two club-lengths from where it first struck a part of the course; or

(vii) rolls and comes to rest nearer the hole than its original position or estimated position (see Rule 20-2b) unless otherwise permitted by the Rules.

If the ball when re-dropped rolls into any position listed above, it shall be placed as near as possible to the spot where it first struck a part of the course when re-dropped.

If a ball to be re-dropped or placed under this Rule is not immediately recoverable, another ball may be substituted.

20-3. Placing and Replacing

a. By Whom and Where

A ball to be placed under the Rules shall be placed by the player or his partner. If a ball is to be replaced, the player, his partner or the person who lifted or moved it shall place it on the spot from which it was lifted or moved. In any such case, the player shall be responsible for any breach of the Rules.

If a ball or the ball-marker is accidentally moved in the process of placing or replacing the ball, the ball or the ball-marker shall be replaced. There is no penalty provided the movement of the ball or the ball-marker is directly attributable to the specific act of placing or replacing the ball or removing the ball-marker. Otherwise, *the player shall incur a penalty stroke* under Rule 18-2a or 20-1.

b. Lie of Ball to Be Placed or Replaced Altered

If the original lie of a ball to be placed or replaced has been altered:

(i) except in a hazard, the ball shall be placed in the nearest lie most similar to the original lie which is not

more than one club-length from the original lie, not nearer the hole and not in a hazard;

(ii) in a water hazard, the ball shall be placed in accordance with Clause (i) above, except that the ball must be placed in the water hazard;

(iii) in a bunker, the original lie shall be recreated as nearly as possible and the ball shall be placed in that lie.

c. Spot Not Determinable

If it is impossible to determine the spot where the ball is to be placed or replaced:

(i) through the green, the ball shall be dropped as near as possible to the place where it lay but not in a hazard;

(ii) in a hazard, the ball shall be dropped in the hazard as near as possible to the place where it lay;

(iii) on the putting green, the ball shall be placed as near as possible to the place where it lay but not in a hazard.

d. Ball Fails to Remain on Spot

If a ball when placed fails to remain on the spot on which it was placed, it shall be replaced without penalty. If it still fails to remain on that spot:

(i) except in a hazard, it shall be placed at the nearest spot not nearer the hole or in a hazard where it can be placed at rest;

(ii) in a hazard, it shall be placed in the hazard at the nearest spot not nearer the hole where it can be placed at rest.

PENALTY FOR BREACH OF RULE 20-1, -2 or -3:
Match play — Loss of hole; Stroke play — Two strokes.

20-4. When Ball Dropped or Placed Is in Play

If the player's ball in play has been lifted, it is again in play when dropped or placed.

A substituted ball becomes the ball in play if it is dropped or placed under an applicable Rule, whether or not such Rule permits substitution. A ball substituted under an inapplicable Rule is a wrong ball.

20-5. Playing Next Stroke from Where Previous Stroke Played

When, under the Rules, a player elects or is required to play his next stroke from where a previous stroke was played, he shall proceed as follows: If the stroke is to be played from the teeing ground, the ball to be played shall be played from anywhere within the teeing ground and may be teed; if the stroke is to be played from through the green or a hazard, it shall be dropped; if the stroke is to be played on the putting green, it shall be placed.

PENALTY FOR BREACH OF RULE 20-5:
Match play — Loss of hole; Stroke play — Two strokes.

20-6. Lifting Ball Wrongly Dropped or Placed

A ball dropped or placed in a wrong place or otherwise not in accordance with the Rules but not played may be lifted, without penalty, and the player shall then proceed correctly.

20-7. Playing from Wrong Place

For a ball played from outside the teeing ground or from a wrong teeing ground — see Rule 11-4 and -5.

a. Match Play

If a player plays a stroke with a ball which has been dropped or placed in a wrong place, *he shall lose the hole.*

b. Stroke Play

If a competitor plays a stroke with (i) his original ball which has been dropped or placed in a wrong place, (ii) a substituted ball which has been dropped or placed under an applicable Rule but in a wrong place or (iii) his ball in play when it has been moved and not replaced in a case where the Rules require replacement, *he shall,* provided a serious breach has not occurred, *incur the penalty prescribed by the applicable Rule* and play out the hole with the ball.

If, after playing from a wrong place, a competitor becomes aware of that fact and believes that a serious breach may be involved, he may, provided he has not played a stroke from the next teeing ground or, in the case of the last hole of the round, left the putting green, declare that he will play out the hole with a second ball dropped or placed in accordance with the Rules. The competitor shall report the facts to the Committee before returning his score card; if he fails to do so, *he shall be disqualified.* The Committee shall determine whether a serious breach of the Rule occurred. If so, the score with the second ball shall count and *the competitor shall add two penalty strokes to his score with that ball.*

If a serious breach has occurred and the competitor has failed to correct it as prescribed above, *he shall be disqualified.*

Note: If a competitor plays a second ball, penalty strokes incurred by playing the ball ruled not to count and strokes subsequently taken with that ball shall be disregarded.

Rule 21. Cleaning Ball

A ball on the putting green may be cleaned when lifted under Rule 16-1b. Elsewhere, a ball may be cleaned when lifted except when it has been lifted:

a. To determine if it is unfit for play (Rule 5-3);

b. For identification (Rule 12-2), in which case it may be cleaned only to the extent necessary for identification; or

c. Because it is interfering with or assisting play (Rule 22).

If a player cleans his ball during play of a hole except as provided in this Rule, *he shall incur a penalty of one stroke* and the ball, if lifted, shall be replaced.

If a player who is required to replace a ball fails to do so, *he shall incur the penalty* for breach of Rule 20-3a, but no additional penalty under Rule 21 shall be applied.

Exception: If a player incurs a penalty for failing to act in accordance with Rule 5-3, 12-2 or 22, no additional penalty under Rule 21 shall be applied.

Rule 22. Ball Interfering with or Assisting Play

Any player may:

a. Lift his ball if he considers that the ball might assist any other player or

b. Have any other ball lifted if he considers that the ball might interfere with his play or assist the play of any other player,

but this may not be done while another ball is in motion. In stroke play, a player required to lift his ball may play first rather than lift. A ball lifted under this Rule shall be replaced.

If a ball is accidentally moved in complying with this Rule, no penalty is incurred and the ball shall be replaced.

PENALTY FOR BREACH OF RULE:
Match play — Loss of hole; Stroke play — Two strokes.

Note: Except on the putting green, the ball may not be cleaned when lifted under this Rule — see Rule 21.

Rule 23. Loose Impediments

"Loose impediments" are natural objects such as stones, leaves, twigs, branches and the like, dung, worms and insects and casts or heaps made by them, provided they are not fixed or growing, are not solidly embedded and do not adhere to the ball.

Sand and loose soil are loose impediments on the putting green but not elsewhere.

Snow and natural ice, other than frost, are either casual water or loose impediments, at the option of the player. Manufactured ice is an obstruction.

Dew and frost are not loose impediments.

23-1. Relief
Except when both the loose impediment and the ball lie in or touch a hazard, any loose impediment may be removed without penalty. If the ball moves, see Rule 18-2c.

When a ball is in motion, a loose impediment which might influence the movement of the ball shall not be removed.

PENALTY FOR BREACH OF RULE:
Match play — Loss of hole; Stroke play — Two strokes.

(Searching for ball in hazard — see Rule 12-1.)
(Touching line of putt — see Rule 16-1a.)

Rule 24. Obstructions

Definition
An "obstruction" is anything artificial, including the artificial surfaces and sides of roads and paths and manufactured ice, except:

a. Objects defining out of bounds, such as walls, fences, stakes and railings;

b. Any part of an immovable artificial object which is out of bounds; and

c. Any construction declared by the Committee to be an integral part of the course.

24-1. Movable Obstruction
A player may obtain relief from a movable obstruction as follows:

a. If the ball does not lie in or on the obstruction, the obstruction may be removed. If the ball moves, it shall be replaced, and there is no penalty provided that the movement of the ball is directly attributable to the removal of the obstruction. Otherwise, Rule 18-2a applies.

b. If the ball lies in or on the obstruction, the ball may be lifted, without penalty, and the obstruction removed. The ball shall through the green or in a hazard be dropped, or on the putting green be placed, as near as possible to the spot directly under the place where the ball lay in or on the obstruction, but not nearer the hole.

The ball may be cleaned when lifted under Rule 24-1.

When a ball is in motion, an obstruction which might influence the movement of the ball, other than an attended flagstick or equipment of the players, shall not be removed.

24-2. Immovable Obstruction
a. INTERFERENCE
Interference by an immovable obstruction occurs when a ball lies in or on the obstruction, or so close to the obstruction that the obstruction interferes with the player's stance or the area of his intended swing. If the player's ball lies on the putting green, interference also occurs if an immovable obstruction on the putting green intervenes on his line of putt. Otherwise, intervention on the line of play is not, of itself, interference under this Rule.

b. RELIEF
Except when the ball lies in or touches a water hazard or a lateral water hazard, a player may obtain relief from interference by an immovable obstruction, without penalty, as follows:

(i) *Through the Green:* If the ball lies through the green, the point on the course nearest to where the ball lies shall be determined (without crossing over, through or under the obstruction) which (a) is not nearer the hole, (b) avoids interference (as defined) and (c) is not in a hazard or on a putting green. The player shall lift the ball and drop it within one club-length of the point thus determined on ground which fulfils (a), (b) and (c) above.

Note: The prohibition against crossing over, through or under the obstruction does not apply to the artificial surfaces and sides of roads and paths or when the ball lies in or on the obstruction.

(ii) *In a Bunker:* If the ball lies in or touches a bunker, the player shall lift and drop the ball in accordance with Clause (i) above, except that the ball must be dropped in the bunker.

(iii) *On the Putting Green:* If the ball lies on the putting green, the player shall lift the ball and place it in the nearest position to where it lay which affords relief from interference, but not nearer the hole nor in a hazard.

The ball may be cleaned when lifted under Rule 24-2b.

(Ball rolling to a position where there is interference by the condition from which relief was taken — see Rule 20-2c(v).)

Exception: A player may not obtain relief under Rule 24-2b if (a) it is clearly unreasonable for him to play a stroke because of interference by anything other than an immovable obstruction or (b) interference by an immovable obstruction would occur only through use of an unnecessarily abnormal stance, swing or direction of play.

Note: If a ball lies in or touches a water hazard (including a lateral water hazard), the player is not entitled to relief without penalty from interference by an immovable obstruction. The player shall play the ball as it lies or proceed under Rule 26-1.

c. BALL LOST

Except in a water hazard or a lateral water hazard, if there is reasonable evidence that a ball is lost in an immovable obstruction, the player may, without penalty, substitute another ball and follow the procedure prescribed in Rule 24-2b. For the purpose of applying this Rule, the ball shall be deemed to lie at the spot where it entered the obstruction. If the ball is lost in an underground drain pipe or culvert the entrance to which is in a hazard, a ball must be dropped in that hazard or the player may proceed under Rule 26-1, if applicable.

PENALTY FOR BREACH OF RULE:
Match play — Loss of hole; Stroke play — Two strokes.

Rule 25. Abnormal Ground Conditions and Wrong Putting Green

"Casual water" is any temporary accumulation of water on the course which is visible before or after the player takes his stance and is not in a water hazard. Snow and natural ice, other than frost, are casual water or loose impediments, at the option of the player. Manufactured ice is an obstruction. Dew and frost are not casual water.

"Ground under repair" is any portion of the course so marked by order of the Committee or so declared by its authorized representative. It includes material piled for removal and a hole made by a greenkeeper, even if not so marked. Stakes and lines defining ground under repair are in such ground. The margin of ground under repair extends vertically downwards, but not upwards.

Note 1: Grass cuttings and other material left on the course which have been abandoned and are not intended to be removed are not ground under repair unless so marked.

Note 2: The Committee may make a Local Rule prohibiting play from ground under repair.

25-1. Casual Water, Ground Under Repair and Certain Damage to Course

a. INTERFERENCE

Interference by casual water, ground under repair or a hole, cast or runway made by a burrowing animal, a reptile or a bird occurs when a ball lies in or touches any of these conditions or when such a condition on the course interferes with the player's stance or the area of his intended swing.

If the player's ball lies on the putting green, interference also occurs if such condition on the putting green intervenes on his line of putt.

If interference exists, the player may either play the ball as it lies (unless prohibited by Local Rule) or take relief as provided in Clause b.

b. RELIEF

If the player elects to take relief, he shall proceed as follows:

(i) *Through the Green:* If the ball lies through the green, the point on the course nearest to where the ball lies shall be determined which (a) is not nearer the hole, (b) avoids interference by the condition, and (c) is not in a hazard or on a putting green. The player shall lift the ball and drop it without penalty within one club-length of the point thus determined on ground which fulfils (a), (b) and (c) above.

(ii) *In a Hazard:* If the ball lies in or touches a hazard, the player shall lift and drop the ball either:

(a) Without penalty, in the hazard, as near as possible to the spot where the ball lay, but not nearer the hole, on ground which affords maximum available relief from the condition;

or

(b) *Under penalty of one stroke,* outside the hazard, keeping the point where the ball lay directly between the hole and the spot on which the ball is dropped.

Exception: If a ball lies in or touches a water hazard (including a lateral water hazard), the player is not entitled to relief without penalty from a hole, cast or runway made by a burrowing animal, a reptile or a bird. The player shall play the ball as it lies or proceed under Rule 26-1.

(iii) *On the Putting Green:* If the ball lies on the putting green, the player shall lift the ball and place it without penalty in the nearest position to where it lay which affords maximum available relief from the condition, but not nearer the hole nor in a hazard.

The ball may be cleaned when lifted under Rule 25-1b.

(Ball rolling to a position where there is interference by the condition from which relief was taken — see Rule 20-2c(v).)

Exception: A player may not obtain relief under Rule 25-1b if (a) it is clearly unreasonable for him to play a stroke because of interference by anything other than a condition covered by Rule 25-1a or (b) interference by such a condition would occur only through use of an unnecessarily abnormal stance, swing or direction of play.

c. BALL LOST UNDER CONDITION COVERED BY RULE 25-1

It is a question of fact whether a ball lost after having been struck toward a condition covered by Rule 25-1 is lost under such condition. In order to treat the ball as lost under such condition, there must be reasonable evidence to that effect. In the absence of such evidence, the ball must be treated as a lost ball and Rule 27 applies.

(i) *Outside a Hazard* — If a ball is lost outside a hazard under a condition covered by Rule 25-1, the player may take relief as follows: the point on the course nearest to where the ball last crossed the margin of the area shall be determined which (a) is not nearer the hole than where the ball last crossed the margin, (b) avoids interference by the condition and (c) is not in a hazard or on a putting green. He shall drop a ball without penalty within one club-length of the point thus determined on ground which fulfils (a), (b) and (c) above.

(ii) *In a Hazard* — If a ball is lost in a hazard under a condition covered by Rule 25-1, the player may drop a ball either:

(a) Without penalty, in the hazard, as near as possible to the point at which the original ball last crossed the margin of the area, but not nearer the hole, on ground which affords maximum available relief from the condition

or

(b) *Under penalty of one stroke*, outside the hazard, keeping the point at which the original ball last crossed the margin of the hazard directly between the hole and the spot on which the ball is dropped.

Exception: If a ball lies in a water hazard (including a lateral water hazard), the player is not entitled to relief without penalty for a ball lost in a hole, cast or runway made by a burrowing animal, a reptile or a bird. The player shall proceed under Rule 26-1.

25-2. Embedded Ball

A ball embedded in its own pitch-mark in the ground in any closely mown area through the green may be lifted, cleaned and dropped, without penalty, as near as possible to the spot where it lay but not nearer the hole. "Closely mown area" means any area of the course, including paths through the rough, cut to fairway height or less.

25-3. Wrong Putting Green

A player must not play a ball which lies on a putting green other than that of the hole being played. The ball must be lifted and the player must proceed as follows: The point on the course nearest to where the ball lies shall be determined which (a) is not nearer the hole and (b) is not in a hazard or on a putting green. The player shall lift the ball and drop it without penalty within one club-length of the point thus determined on ground which fulfils (a) and (b) above. The ball may be cleaned when so lifted.

Note: Unless otherwise prescribed by the Committee, the term "a putting green other than that of the hole being played" includes a practice putting green or pitching green on the course.

PENALTY FOR BREACH OF RULE:
Match play — Loss of hole; Stroke play — Two strokes.

Rule 26. Water Hazards (Including Lateral Water Hazards)

Definitions

A "water hazard" is any sea, lake, pond, river, ditch, surface drainage ditch or other open water course (whether or not containing water) and anything of a similar nature.

All ground or water within the margin of a water hazard is part of the water hazard. The margin of a water hazard extends vertically upwards and downwards. Stakes and lines defining the margins of water hazards are in the hazards.

Note: Water hazards (other than lateral water hazards) should be defined by yellow stakes or lines.

A "lateral water hazard" is a water hazard or that part of a water hazard so situated that it is not possible or is deemed by the Committee to be impracticable to drop a ball behind the water hazard in accordance with Rule 26-1b.

That part of a water hazard to be played as a lateral water hazard should be distinctively marked.

Note: Lateral water hazards should be defined by red stakes or lines.

26-1. Ball In Water Hazard

It is a question of fact whether a ball lost after having been struck toward a water hazard is lost inside or outside the hazard. In order to treat the ball as lost in the hazard, there must be reasonable evidence that the ball lodged in it. In the absence of such evidence, the ball must be treated as a lost ball and Rule 27 applies.

If a ball lies in, touches or is lost in a water hazard (whether the ball lies in water or not), the player may *under penalty of one stroke:*

a. Play a ball as nearly as possible at the spot from which the original ball was last played (see Rule 20-5);

or

b. Drop a ball behind the water hazard, keeping the point at which the original ball last crossed the margin of the water hazard directly between the hole and the spot on which the ball is dropped, with no limit to how far behind the water hazard the ball may be dropped.

or

c. *As additional options available only if the ball lies in, touches or is lost in a lateral water hazard,* drop a ball outside the water hazard within two club-lengths of (i) the point where the original ball last crossed the margin of the water hazard or (ii) a point on the opposite margin of the water hazard equidistant from the hole. The ball must be dropped and come to rest not nearer the hole than the point where the original ball last crossed the margin of the water hazard.

The ball may be cleaned when lifted under this Rule.

(Ball moving in water in a water hazard — see Rule 14-6.)

26-2. Ball Played Within Water Hazard

a. BALL COMES TO REST IN HAZARD

If a ball played from within a water hazard comes to rest in the hazard after the stroke, the player may:

(i) proceed under Rule 26-1; or

(ii) *under penalty of one stroke*, play a ball as nearly as possible at the spot from which the last stroke from outside the hazard was played (see Rule 20-5).

If the player proceeds under Rule 26-1a, he may elect not to play the dropped ball. If he so elects, he may:

a. Proceed under Rule 26-1b, *adding the additional penalty of one stroke* prescribed by that Rule;

or

b. Proceed under Rule 26-1c, if applicable, *adding the additional penalty of one stroke* prescribed by that Rule;

or

c. *Add an additional penalty of one stroke* and play a ball as nearly as possible at the spot from which the last stroke from outside the hazard was played (see Rule 20-5).

b. BALL LOST OR UNPLAYABLE OUTSIDE HAZARD OR OUT OF BOUNDS

If a ball played from within a water hazard is lost or declared unplayable outside the hazard or is out of bounds, the player, after taking *a penalty of one stroke* under Rule 27-1 or 28a, may:

(i) play a ball as nearly as possible at the spot in the hazard from which the original ball was last played (see Rule 20-5); or

(ii) proceed under Rule 26-1b, or if applicable Rule 26-1c, *adding the additional penalty of one stroke* prescribed by the Rule and using as the reference point the point where the original ball last crossed the margin of the hazard before it came to rest in the hazard; or

(iii) *add an additional penalty of one stroke* and play a ball as nearly as possible at the spot from which the last stroke from outside the hazard was played (see Rule 20-5).

Note 1: When proceeding under Rule 26-2b, the player is not required to drop a ball under Rule 27-1 or 28a. If he does drop a ball, he is not required to play it. He may alternatively proceed under Clause (ii) or (iii).

Note 2: If a ball played from within a water hazard is declared unplayable outside the hazard, nothing in Rule 26-2b precludes the player from proceeding under Rule 28b or c.

PENALTY FOR BREACH OF RULE:
Match play — Loss of hole; Stroke play — Two strokes.

Rule 27. Ball Lost or Out of Bounds; Provisional Ball

If the original ball is lost in an immovable obstruction (Rule 24-2) or under a condition covered by Rule 25-1 (casual water, ground under repair and certain damage to the course), the player may proceed under the applicable Rule. If the original ball is lost in a water hazard, the player shall proceed under Rule 26.

Such Rules may not be used unless there is reasonable evidence that the ball is lost in an immovable obstruction, under a condition covered by Rule 25-1 or in a water hazard.

Definitions
A ball is "lost" if:

a. It is not found or identified as his by the player within five minutes after the player's side or his or their caddies have begun to search for it; or

b. The player has put another ball into play under the Rules, even though he may not have searched for the original ball; or

c. The player has played any stroke with a provisional ball from the place where the original ball is likely to be or from a point nearer the hole than that place, whereupon the provisional ball becomes the ball in play.

Time spent in playing a wrong ball is not counted in the five-minute period allowed for search.

"Out of bounds" is ground on which play is prohibited.

When out of bounds is defined by reference to stakes or a fence, or as being beyond stakes or a fence, the out of bounds line is determined by the nearest inside points of the stakes or fence posts at ground level excluding angled supports.

When out of bounds is defined by a line on the ground, the line itself is out of bounds.

The out of bounds line extends vertically upwards and downwards.

A ball is out of bounds when all of it lies out of bounds.

A player may stand out of bounds to play a ball lying within bounds.

A "provisional ball" is a ball played under Rule 27-2 for a ball which may be lost outside a water hazard or may be out of bounds.

27-1. Ball Lost or Out of Bounds
If a ball is lost outside a water hazard or is out of bounds, the player shall play a ball, *under penalty of one stroke,* as nearly as possible at the spot from which the original ball was last played (see Rule 20-5).

PENALTY FOR BREACH OF RULE 27-1:
Match play — Loss of hole; Stroke play — Two strokes.

27-2. Provisional Ball

a. PROCEDURE
If a ball may be lost outside a water hazard or may be out of bounds, to save time the player may play another ball provisionally as nearly as possible at the spot from which the original ball was played (see Rule 20-5). The player shall inform his opponent in match play or his marker or a fellow-competitor in stroke play that he intends to play a provisional ball, and he shall play it before he or his partner goes forward to search for the original ball. If he fails to do so and plays another ball, such ball is not a provisional ball and becomes the ball in play *under penalty of stroke and distance* (Rule 27-1); the original ball is deemed to be lost.

b. WHEN PROVISIONAL BALL BECOMES BALL IN PLAY
The player may play a provisional ball until he reaches the place where the original ball is likely to be. If he plays a stroke with the provisional ball from the place where the original ball is likely to be or from a point nearer the hole than that place, the original ball is deemed to be lost and the provisional ball becomes the ball in play *under penalty of stroke and distance* (Rule 27-1).

If the original ball is lost outside a water hazard or is out of bounds, the provisional ball becomes the ball in play, *under penalty of stroke and distance* (Rule 27-1).

c. WHEN PROVISIONAL BALL TO BE ABANDONED
If the original ball is neither lost outside a water hazard nor out of bounds, the player shall abandon the provisional ball and continue play with the original ball. If he fails to do so, any further strokes played with the provisional ball shall constitute playing a wrong ball and the provisions of Rule 15 shall apply.

Note: If the original ball lies in a water hazard, the player shall play the ball as it lies or proceed under Rule 26. If it is lost in a water hazard or unplayable, the player shall proceed under Rule 26 or 28, whichever is applicable.

Rule 28. Ball Unplayable

The player may declare his ball unplayable at any place on the course except when the ball lies in or touches a water hazard. The player is the sole judge as to whether his ball is unplayable.

If the player deems his ball to be unplayable, he shall, *under penalty of one stroke:*

a. Play a ball as nearly as possible at the spot from which the original ball was last played (see Rule 20-5); or

b. Drop a ball within two club-lengths of the spot where the ball lay, but not nearer the hole; or

c. Drop a ball behind the point where the ball lay, keeping that point directly between the hole and the spot on which the ball is dropped, with no limit to how far behind that point the ball may be dropped.

If the unplayable ball lies in a bunker, the player may proceed under Clause a, b or c. If he elects to proceed under Clause b or c, a ball must be dropped in the bunker.

The ball may be cleaned when lifted under this Rule.

PENALTY FOR BREACH OF RULE:
Match play — Loss of hole; Stroke play — Two strokes.

OTHER FORMS OF PLAY
Rule 29. Threesomes and Foursomes
Definitions
Threesome: A match in which one plays against two, and each side plays one ball.

Foursome: A match in which two play against two, and each side plays one ball.

29-1. General

In a threesome or a foursome, during any stipulated round the partners shall play alternately from the teeing grounds and alternately during the play of each hole. Penalty strokes do not affect the order of play.

29-2. Match Play

If a player plays when his partner should have played, *his side shall lose the hole.*

29-3. Stroke Play

If the partners play a stroke or strokes in incorrect order, such stroke or strokes shall be cancelled and *the side shall incur a penalty of two strokes.* The side shall correct the error by playing a ball in correct order as nearly as possible at the spot from which it first played in incorrect order (see Rule 20-5). If the side plays a stroke from the next teeing ground without first correcting the error or, in the case of the last hole of the round, leaves the putting green without declaring its intention to correct the error, *the side shall be disqualified.*

Rule 30. Three-Ball, Best-Ball and Four-Ball Match Play

Definitions

Three-Ball: A match play competition in which three play against one another, each playing his own ball. Each player is playing two distinct matches.

Best-Ball: A match in which one plays against the better ball of two or the best ball of three players.

Four-Ball: A match in which two play their better ball against the better ball of two other players.

30-1. Rules of Golf Apply

The Rules of Golf, so far as they are not at variance with the following special Rules, shall apply to three-ball, best-ball and four-ball matches.

30-2. Three-Ball Match Play

a. BALL AT REST MOVED BY AN OPPONENT

Except as otherwise provided in the Rules, if the player's ball is touched or moved by an opponent, his caddie or equipment other than during search, Rule 18-3b applies. *That opponent shall incur a penalty stroke in his match with the player,* but not in his match with the other opponent.

b. BALL DEFLECTED OR STOPPED BY AN OPPONENT ACCIDENTALLY

If a player's ball is accidentally deflected or stopped by an opponent, his caddie or equipment, no penalty shall be incurred. In his match with that opponent the player may play the ball as it lies or, before another stroke is played by either side, he may cancel the stroke and play a ball without penalty as nearly as possible at the spot from which the original ball was last played (see Rule 20-5). In his match with the other opponent, the ball shall be played as it lies.

Exception: Ball striking person attending flagstick — see Rule 17-3b.

(Ball purposely deflected or stopped by opponent — see Rule 1-2.)

30-3. Best-Ball and Four-Ball Match Play

a. REPRESENTATION OF SIDE

A side may be represented by one partner for all or any part of a match; all partners need not be present. An absent partner may join a match between holes, but not during play of a hole.

b. MAXIMUM OF FOURTEEN CLUBS

The side shall be penalized for a breach of Rule 4-4 by any partner.

c. ORDER OF PLAY

Balls belonging to the same side may be played in the order the side considers best.

d. WRONG BALL

If a player plays a stroke with a wrong ball except in a hazard, *he shall be disqualified for that hole,* but his partner incurs no penalty even if the wrong ball belongs to him. If the wrong ball belongs to another player, its owner shall place a ball on the spot from which the wrong ball was first played.

e. DISQUALIFICATION OF SIDE

(i) *A side shall be disqualified* for a breach of any of the following by any partner:

Rule 1-3 — Agreement to Waive Rules.
Rule 4-1, -2 or -3 — Clubs.
Rule 5-1 or -2 — The Ball.
Rule 6-2a — Handicap (playing off higher handicap).
Rule 6-4 — Caddie.
Rule 6-7 — Undue Delay (repeated offense).
Rule 14-3 — Artificial Devices and Unusual Equipment.

(ii) *A side shall be disqualified* for a breach of any of the following by all partners:

Rule 6-3 — Time of Starting and Groups.
Rule 6-8 — Discontinuance of Play.

f. EFFECT OF OTHER PENALTIES

If a player's breach of a Rule assists his partner's play or adversely affects an opponent's play, *the partner incurs the applicable penalty in addition to any penalty incurred by the player.*

In all other cases where a player incurs a penalty for breach of a Rule, the penalty shall not apply to his partner. Where the penalty is stated to be loss of hole, the effect shall be to disqualify the player for that hole.

g. ANOTHER FORM OF MATCH PLAYED CONCURRENTLY

In a best-ball or four-ball match when another form of match is played concurrently, the above special Rules shall apply.

Rule 31. Four-Ball Stroke Play

In four-ball stroke play two competitors play as partners, each playing his own ball. The lower score of the partners is the score for the hole. If one partner fails to complete the play of a hole, there is no penalty.

31-1. Rules of Golf Apply

The Rules of Golf, so far as they are not at variance with the following special Rules, shall apply to four-ball stroke play.

31-2. Representation of Side

A side may be represented by either partner for all or any part of a stipulated round; both partners need not be present. An absent competitor may join his partner between holes, but not during play of a hole.

31-3. Maximum of Fourteen Clubs

The side shall be penalized for a breach of Rule 4-4 by either partner.

31-4. Scoring

The marker is required to record for each hole only the gross score of whichever partner's score is to count. The gross scores to count must be individually identifiable; otherwise *the side shall be disqualified.* Only one of the partners need be responsible for complying with Rule 6-6b.

(Wrong score — see Rule 31-7a.)

31-5. Order of Play
Balls belonging to the same side may be played in the order the side considers best.

31-6. Wrong Ball
If a competitor plays a stroke with a <u>wrong ball</u> except in a <u>hazard</u>, *he shall add two penalty strokes to his score for the hole* and shall then play the correct ball. His partner incurs no penalty even if the wrong ball belongs to him.

If the wrong ball belongs to another competitor, its owner shall place a ball on the spot from which the wrong ball was first played.

31-7. Disqualification Penalties

a. BREACH BY ONE PARTNER
A side shall be disqualified from the competition for a breach of any of the following by either partner:
Rule 1-3 — Agreement to Waive Rules.
Rule 3-4 — Refusal to Comply with Rule.
Rule 4-1, -2 or -3 — Clubs.
Rule 5-1 or -2 — The Ball.
Rule 6-2b — Handicap (playing off higher handicap; failure to record handicap).
Rule 6-4 — Caddie.
Rule 6-6b — Signing and Returning Card.
Rule 6-6d — Wrong Score for Hole, *i.e.*, when the recorded score of the partner whose score is to count is lower than actually taken. If the recorded score of the partner whose score is to count is higher than actually taken, it must stand as returned.
Rule 6-7 — Undue Delay (repeated offense).
Rule 7-1 — Practice Before or Between Rounds.
Rule 14-3 — Artificial Devices and Unusual Equipment.
Rule 31-4 — Gross Scores to Count Not Individually Identifiable.

b. BREACH BY BOTH PARTNERS
A side shall be disqualified:
(i) for a breach by both partners of Rule 6-3 (Time of Starting and Groups) or Rule 6-8 (Discontinuance of Play), or
(ii) if, at the same hole, each partner is in breach of a Rule the penalty for which is disqualification from the competition or for a hole.

c. FOR THE HOLE ONLY
In all other cases where a breach of a Rule would entail disqualification, *the competitor shall be disqualified only for the hole at which the breach occurred.*

31-8. Effect of Other Penalties
If a competitor's breach of a Rule assists his partner's play, *the partner incurs the applicable penalty in addition to any penalty incurred by the competitor.*

In all other cases where a competitor incurs a penalty for breach of a Rule, the penalty shall not apply to his partner.

Rule 32. Bogey, Par and Stableford Competitions

32-1. Conditions
Bogey, par and Stableford competitions are forms of stroke competition in which play is against a fixed score at each hole. The Rules for stroke play, so far as they are not at variance with the following special Rules, apply.

a. BOGEY AND PAR COMPETITIONS
The reckoning for bogey and par competitions is made as in match play. Any hole for which a competitor makes no return shall be regarded as a loss. The winner is the competitor who is most successful in the aggregate of holes.

The marker is responsible for marking only the gross number of strokes for each hole where the competitor makes a net score equal to or less than the fixed score.

Note: Maximum of 14 clubs — Penalties as in match play — see Rule 4-4.

b. STABLEFORD COMPETITIONS
The reckoning in Stableford competitions is made by points awarded in relation to a fixed score at each hole as follows:

Hole Played In	Points
More than one over fixed score or no score returned	0
One over fixed score	1
Fixed score	2
One under fixed score	3
Two under fixed score	4
Three under fixed score	5
Four under fixed score	6

The winner is the competitor who scores the highest number of points.

The marker shall be responsible for marking only the gross number of strokes at each hole where the competitor's net score earns one or more points.

Note: Maximum of 14 clubs (Rule 4-4) — Penalties applied as follows: From total points scored for the round, deduction of two points for each hole at which any breach occurred; maximum deduction per round: four points.

32-2. Disqualification Penalties

a. FROM THE COMPETITION
A competitor shall be disqualified from the competition for a breach of any of the following:
Rule 1-3 — Agreement to Waive Rules.
Rule 3-4 — Refusal to Comply with Rule.
Rule 4-1, -2 or -3 — Clubs.
Rule 5-1 or -2 — The Ball.
Rule 6-2b — Handicap (playing off higher handicap; failure to record handicap).
Rule 6-3 — Time of Starting and Groups.
Rule 6-4 — Caddie.
Rule 6-6b — Signing and Returning Card.
Rule 6-6d — Wrong Score for Hole, except that no penalty shall be incurred when a breach of this Rule does not affect the result of the hole.
Rule 6-7 — Undue Delay (repeated offense).
Rule 6-8 — Discontinuance of Play.
Rule 7-1 — Practice Before or Between Rounds.
Rule 14-3 — Artificial Devices and Unusual Equipment.

b. FOR A HOLE
In all other cases where a breach of a Rule would entail disqualification, *the competitor shall be disqualified only for the hole at which the breach occurred.*

ADMINISTRATION
Rule 33. The Committee

33-1. Conditions; Waiving Rule
The Committee shall lay down the conditions under which a competition is to be played.

The Committee has no power to waive a Rule of Golf.

Certain special rules governing stroke play are so substantially different from those governing match play that combining the two forms of play is not practicable and is not permitted. The results of matches played and the scores returned in these circumstances shall not be accepted.

In stroke play the Committee may limit a referee's duties.

33-2. The Course

a. DEFINING BOUNDS AND MARGINS

The Committee shall define accurately:
   (i) the course and out of bounds,
   (ii) the margins of water hazards and lateral water hazards,
   (iii) ground under repair, and
   (iv) obstructions and integral parts of the course.

b. NEW HOLES

New holes should be made on the day on which a stroke competition begins and at such other times as the Committee considers necessary, provided all competitors in a single round play with each hole cut in the same position.

Exception: When it is impossible for a damaged hole to be repaired so that it conforms with the Definition, the Committee may make a new hole in a nearby similar position.

c. PRACTICE GROUND

Where there is no practice ground available outside the area of a competition course, the Committee should lay down the area on which players may practice on any day of a competition, if it is practicable to do so. On any day of a stroke competition, the Committee should not normally permit practice on or to a putting green or from a hazard of the competition course.

d. COURSE UNPLAYABLE

If the Committee or its authorized representative considers that for any reason the course is not in a playable condition or that there are circumstances which render the proper playing of the game impossible, it may, in match play or stroke play, order a temporary suspension of play or, in stroke play, declare play null and void and cancel all scores for the round in question. When play has been temporarily suspended, it shall be resumed from where it was discontinued, even though resumption occurs on a subsequent day. When a round is cancelled, all penalties incurred in that round are cancelled.

(Procedure in discontinuing play — see Rule 6-8.)

33-3. Times of Starting and Groups

The Committee shall lay down the times of starting and, in stroke play, arrange the groups in which competitors shall play.

When a match play competition is played over an extended period, the Committee shall lay down the limit of time within which each round shall be completed. When players are allowed to arrange the date of their match within these limits, the Committee should announce that the match must be played at a stated time on the last day of the period unless the players agree to a prior date.

33-4. Handicap Stroke Table

The Committee shall publish a table indicating the order of holes at which handicap strokes are to be given or received.

33-5. Score Card

In stroke play, the Committee shall issue for each competitor a score card containing the date and the competitor's name or, in foursome or four-ball stroke play, the competitors' names.

In stroke play, the Committee is responsible for the addition of scores and application of the handicap recorded on the card.

In four-ball stroke play, the Committee is responsible for recording the better-ball score for each hole and in the process applying the handicaps recorded on the card, and adding the better-ball scores.

In bogey, par and Stableford competitions, the Committee is responsible for applying the handicap recorded on the card and determining the result of each hole and the overall result or points total.

33-6. Decision of Ties

The Committee shall announce the manner, day and time for the decision of a halved match or of a tie, whether played on level terms or under handicap.

A halved match shall not be decided by stroke play. A tie in stroke play shall not be decided by a match.

33-7. Disqualification Penalty; Committee Discretion

A penalty of disqualification may in exceptional individual cases be waived, modified or imposed if the Committee considers such action warranted.

Any penalty less than disqualification shall not be waived or modified.

33-8. Local Rules

a. POLICY

The Committee may make and publish Local Rules for abnormal conditions if they are consistent with the policy of the Governing Authority for the country concerned as set forth in Appendix I to these Rules.

b. WAIVING PENALTY

A penalty imposed by a Rule of Golf shall not be waived by a Local Rule.

Rule 34. Disputes and Decisions

34-1. Claims and Penalties

a. MATCH PLAY

In match play if a claim is lodged with the Committee under Rule 2-5, a decision should be given as soon as possible so that the state of the match may, if necessary, be adjusted.

If a claim is not made within the time limit provided by Rule 2-5, it shall not be considered unless it is based on facts previously unknown to the player making the claim and the player making the claim had been given wrong information (Rules 6-2a and 9) by an opponent. In any case, no later claim shall be considered after the result of the match has been officially announced, unless the Committee is satisfied that the opponent knew he was giving wrong information.

b. STROKE PLAY

In stroke play no penalty shall be rescinded, modified or imposed after the competition has closed, except that a penalty of disqualification shall be imposed at any time after the competition has closed if a competitor:
   (i) returned a score for any hole lower than actually taken (Rule 6-6d) for any reason other than failure to include a penalty which he did not know he had incurred; or
   (ii) returned a score card on which he had recorded a handicap which he knew was higher than that to which he was entitled, and this affected the number of strokes received (Rule 6-2b); or
   (iii) was in breach of Rule 1-3.

A competition is deemed to have closed when the result has been officially announced or, in stroke play qualifying followed by match play, when the player has teed off in his first match.

34-2. Referee's Decision

If a referee has been appointed by the Committee, his decision shall be final.

34-3. Committee's Decision

In the absence of a referee, any dispute or doubtful point on the Rules shall be referred to the Committee, whose decision shall be final.

If the Committee cannot come to a decision, it shall refer the dispute or doubtful point to the Rules of Golf Committee of the United States Golf Association, whose decision shall be final.

If the dispute or doubtful point has not been referred to the Rules of Golf Committee, the player or players have the right to refer an agreed statement through the Secretary of the Club to the Rules of Golf Committee for an opinion as to the correctness of the decision given. The reply will be sent to the Secretary of the Club or Clubs concerned.

If play is conducted other than in accordance with the Rules of Golf, the Rules of Golf Committee will not give a decision on any question.

Appendix I
LOCAL RULES;
CONDITIONS OF THE COMPETITION
Local Rules

Rule 33-8 provides:

"The Committee may make and publish Local Rules for abnormal conditions if they are consistent with the policy of the Governing Authority for the country concerned as set forth in Appendix I to these Rules.

"A penalty imposed by a Rule of Golf shall not be waived by a Local Rule."

Information regarding acceptable and prohibited Local Rules is provided in the *Decisions on the Rules of Golf* under Rule 33-8. Among the matters for which Local Rules may be advisable are the following:

1. Obstructions
Clarifying the status of objects which may be obstructions (Rule 24).

Declaring any construction to be an integral part of the course and, accordingly, not an obstruction, *e.g.*, built-up sides of teeing grounds, putting greens and bunkers (Rules 24 and 33-2a).

2. Roads and Paths
Providing relief of the type afforded under Rule 24-2b from roads and paths not having artificial surfaces and sides if they could unfairly affect play.

3. Preservation of Course
Preservation of the course by defining areas, including turf nurseries and other parts of the course under cultivation, as ground under repair from which play is prohibited.

4. Water Hazards
Lateral Water Hazards. Clarifying the status of sections of water hazards which may be lateral water hazards (Rule 26).

Provisional Ball. Permitting play of a provisional ball for a ball which may be in a water hazard of such character that it would be impracticable to determine whether the ball is in the hazard or to do so would unduly delay play. In such case, if a provisional ball is played and the original ball is in a water hazard, the player may play the original ball as it lies or continue the provisional ball in play, but he may not proceed under Rule 26-1.

5. Defining Bounds and Margins
Specifying means used to define out of bounds, hazards, water hazards, lateral water hazards and ground under repair.

6. Ball Drops
Establishment of special areas on which balls may be dropped when it is not feasible or practicable to proceed exactly in conformity with Rule 24-2b (immovable obstructions), Rule 25-1b or -1c (ground under repair), Rule 26-1 (water hazards and lateral water hazards) and Rule 28 (ball unplayable).

7. Temporary Conditions — Mud, Extreme Wetness
Temporary conditions which might interfere with proper playing of the game, including mud and extreme wetness warranting lifting an embedded ball anywhere through the green (see detailed recommendation below) or removal of mud from a ball through the green.

* * *

Following are the suggested texts for other Local Rules which are authorized by the USGA:

Lifting an Embedded Ball
Rule 25-2 provides relief without penalty for a ball embedded in its own pitch-mark in any closely mown area through the green.

On the putting green, a ball may be lifted and damage caused by the impact of a ball may be repaired (Rules 16-1b and c).

When permission to lift an embedded ball anywhere through the green would be warranted, the following Local Rule is suggested:

Anywhere "through the green," a ball which is embedded in its own pitch-mark in the ground, except in loose sand, may be lifted without penalty, cleaned and dropped as near as possible to the spot where it lay but not nearer the hole. (See Rule 20.)

("Through the green" is the whole area of the course except:

a. Teeing ground and putting green of the hole being played;

b. All hazards on the course.)

Exception: A player may not obtain relief under this Rule if it is clearly unreasonable for him to play a stroke because of interference by anything other than the condition covered by this Rule.

Practice Between Holes
When, between the play of two holes, it is desired to prohibit practice putting or chipping on or near the putting green of the hole last played, the following Local Rule is recommended:

Between the play of two holes, a player shall not play any practice stroke on or near the putting green of the hole last played. (For other practice, see Rules 7 and 33-2c.)

PENALTY FOR BREACH OF LOCAL RULE:
Match play — Loss of next hole; Stroke play — Two strokes at next hole.

Marking Position of Lifted Ball
When it is desired to require a specific means of marking the position of a lifted ball on the putting green, the following Local Rule is recommended:

Before a ball on the putting green is lifted, its position shall be marked by placing a small coin or some similar object immediately behind the ball; if the ball-marker interferes with another player, it should be moved one or more putterhead-lengths to one side. If the position of the ball is not so marked, *the player shall incur a penalty of one stroke* and the ball shall be replaced. If the ball is not replaced, *the player shall incur the penalty* for breach of Rule 20-3a, but no additional penalty under this Local Rule shall be applied. (This modifies Rule 20-1.)

Prohibition Against
Touching Line of Putt with Club
When it is desired to prohibit touching the line of putt with a club in moving loose impediments, the following Local Rule is recommended:

The line of putt shall not be touched with a club for any purpose except to repair old hole plugs or ball marks or during address. (This modifies Rule 16-1a.)

PENALTY FOR BREACH OF LOCAL RULE:
Match play — Loss of hole; Stroke play — Two strokes.

Protection of Young Trees

When it is desired to prevent damage to young trees, the following Local Rule is recommended:

Protection of young trees identified by _____ — If such a tree interferes with a player's stance or the area of his intended swing, the ball must be lifted, without penalty, and dropped in accordance with the procedure prescribed in Rule 24-2b(i) (Immovable Obstruction). The ball may be cleaned when so lifted.

Temporary Obstructions

When temporary obstructions are installed for a competition, the following Local Rule is recommended:

1. Definition

Temporary immovable obstructions include tents, scoreboards, grandstands, refreshment stands and lavatories. Any temporary equipment for photography, press, radio and television is also a temporary immovable obstruction, provided it is not mobile or otherwise readily movable.

Excluded are temporary power lines and cables and mats covering them and temporary telephone lines and stanchions supporting them (from which relief is provided in Clause 5) and mobile or otherwise readily movable equipment for photography, press, radio or television (from which relief is obtainable under Rule 24-1).

2. Interference

Interference by a temporary immovable obstruction occurs when (a) the ball lies in or on the obstruction or so close to the obstruction that the obstruction interferes with the player's stance or the area of his intended swing or (b) the obstruction intervenes between the player's ball and the hole or the ball lies within one club-length of a spot where such intervention would exist.

3. Relief

A player may obtain relief from interference by a temporary immovable obstruction as follows:

a. THROUGH THE GREEN

Through the green, the point on the course nearest to where the ball lies shall be determined which (a) is not nearer the hole, (b) avoids interference as defined in Clause 2 of this Local Rule and (c) is not in a hazard or on a putting green. He shall lift the ball and drop it without penalty within one club-length of the point thus determined on ground which fulfils (a), (b) and (c) above. The ball may be cleaned when so lifted.

b. IN A HAZARD

If the ball lies in a hazard, the player shall lift and drop the ball either:

(i) in the hazard, without penalty, on the nearest ground affording complete relief within the limits specified in Clause 3a above or, if complete relief is impossible, on ground within the hazard affording maximum relief, or

(ii) outside the hazard, *under penalty of one stroke*, as follows: The player shall determine the point on the course nearest to where the ball lies which (a) is not nearer the hole, (b) avoids interference as defined in Clause 2 of this Local Rule and (c) is not in a hazard. He shall drop the ball within one club-length of the point thus determined on ground which fulfils (a), (b) and (c) above.
The ball may be cleaned when so lifted.

Exception: A player may not obtain relief from a temporary immovable obstruction under Clause 3a or 3b if (a) it is clearly unreasonable for him to play a stroke, or in the case of intervention to play a stroke directly toward the obstruction, because of interference by anything other than the obstruction or (b) interference would

occur only through use of an unnecessarily abnormal stance, swing or direction of play.

4. Ball Lost in Temporary Immovable Obstruction

If there is reasonable evidence that a ball is lost within the confines of a temporary immovable obstruction, the player may take relief without penalty as prescribed in Rule 24-2c.

5. Temporary Power Lines and Cables

The above Clauses do not apply to (1) temporary power lines or cables or mats covering them or (2) temporary telephone lines or stanchions supporting them. If such items are readily movable, the player may obtain relief under Rule 24-1. If they are not readily movable, the player may, if the ball lies through the green, obtain relief as provided in Rule 24-2b(i). If the ball lies in a bunker or a water hazard, the player may obtain relief under Rule 24-2b(i), except that the ball must be dropped in the bunker or water hazard.

Note: The prohibition in Rule 24-2b(i) against crossing over, through or under the obstruction does not apply.

If a ball strikes a temporary power line or cable which is elevated, it must be replayed, without penalty (see Rule 20-5). If the ball is not immediately recoverable, another ball may be substituted.

Exception: Ball striking elevated junction section of cable rising from the ground shall not be replayed.

6. Re-Dropping

If a dropped ball rolls into a position covered by this Local Rule, or nearer the hole than its original position, it shall be re-dropped without penalty. If it again rolls into such a position, it shall be placed where it first struck a part of the course when re-dropped.

PENALTY FOR BREACH OF LOCAL RULE:
Match play — Loss of hole; Stroke play — Two strokes.

"Preferred Lies" and "Winter Rules"

The USGA does not endorse "preferred lies" and "winter rules" and recommends that the Rules of Golf be observed uniformly. Ground under repair is provided for in Rule 25. Occasional abnormal conditions which might interfere with fair play and are not widespread should be defined accurately as ground under repair.

However, adverse conditions are sometimes so general throughout a course that the Committee believes "preferred lies" or "winter rules" would promote fair play or help protect the course. Heavy snows, spring thaws, prolonged rains or extreme heat can make fairways unsatisfactory and sometimes prevent use of heavy mowing equipment.

When a Committee adopts a Local Rule for "preferred lies" or "winter rules," it should be in detail and should be interpreted by the Committee, as there is no established code for "winter rules." Without a detailed Local Rule, it is meaningless for a Committee to post a notice merely saying "Winter Rules Today."

The following Local Rule would seem appropriate for the conditions in question, but the USGA will not interpret it:

A ball lying on a "fairway" may be lifted and cleaned, without penalty, and placed within one club-length of where it originally lay, not nearer the hole, and so as to preserve as nearly as possible the stance required to play from the original lie. A ball so lifted is back in play when the player addresses it or, if he does not address it, when he makes his next stroke at it.

Before a Committee adopts a Local Rule permitting "preferred lies" or "winter rules," the following facts should be considered:

1. Such a Local Rule conflicts with the Rules of Golf and the fundamental principle of playing the ball as it lies.

2. "Winter rules" are sometimes adopted under the guise of protecting the course when, in fact, the practical effect is just the opposite — they permit moving the ball to the best turf, from which divots are then taken to injure the course further.

3. "Preferred lies" or "winter rules" tend generally to lower scores and handicaps, thus penalizing the players in competition with players whose scores for handicaps are made under the Rules of Golf.

4. Extended use or indiscriminate use of "preferred lies" or "winter rules" will place players at a disadvantage when competing at a course where the ball must be played as it lies.

Handicapping and "Preferred Lies"

Scores made under a Local Rule for "preferred lies" or "winter rules" may be accepted for handicapping if the Committee considers that conditions warrant.

When such a Local Rule is adopted, the Committee should ensure that the course's normal scoring difficulty is maintained as nearly as possible through adjustment of tee-markers and related methods. However, if extreme conditions cause extended use of "preferred lies" or "winter rules" and the course management cannot adjust scoring difficulty properly, the club should obtain a Temporary Course Rating from its district golf association.

Conditions of the Competition

Rule 33-1 states: "The Committee shall lay down the conditions under which a competition is to be played." Conditions should include such matters as method of entry, eligibility requirements, format, the method of deciding ties, the method of determining the draw for match play and handicap allowances for a handicap competition.

How to Decide Ties

Rule 33-6 empowers the Committee to determine how and when a halved match or a stroke play tie shall be decided. The decision should be published in advance.
The USGA recommends:

1. Match Play

A match which ends all square should be played off hole by hole until one side wins a hole. The play-off should start on the hole where the match began. In a handicap match, handicap strokes should be allowed as in the prescribed round.

2. Stroke Play

(a) In the event of a tie in a scratch stroke play competition, an 18-hole play-off is recommended. If that is not feasible, a hole-by-hole play-off is recommended.

(b) In the event of a tie in a handicap stroke play competition, a play-off over 18 holes with handicaps is recommended. If a shorter play-off is necessary, the percentage of 18 holes to be played should be applied to the players' handicaps to determine their play-off handicaps. It is advisable to arrange for a percentage of holes that will result in whole numbers in handicaps; if this is not feasible, handicap stroke fractions of one-half stroke or more should count as a full stroke and any lesser fraction should be disregarded.

(c) In either a scratch or handicap stroke play competition, if a play-off of any type is not feasible, matching score cards is recommended. The method of matching cards should be announced in advance. An acceptable method of matching cards is to determine the winner on the basis of the best score for the last nine holes. If the tying players have the same score for the last nine, determine the winner on the basis of the last six holes, last three holes and finally the 18th hole. If such a method is used in a handicap stroke play competition, one-half, one-third, one-sixth, etc. of the handicaps should be deducted.

(d) If the conditions of the competition provide that ties shall be decided over the last nine, last six, last three and last hole, they should also provide what will happen if this procedure does not produce a winner.

Draw for Match Play

Although the draw for match play may be completely blind or certain players may be distributed through different quarters or eighths, the General Numerical Draw is recommended if flights are determined by a qualifying round.

General Numerical Draw

For purposes of determining places in the draw, ties in qualifying rounds other than those for the last qualifying place shall be decided by the order in which scores are returned, the first score to be returned receiving the lowest available number, etc. If it is impossible to determine the order in which scores are returned, ties shall be determined by a blind draw.

Upper Half	Lower Half	Upper Half	Lower Half
64 Qualifiers		32 Qualifiers	
1 vs. 64	2 vs. 63	1 vs. 32	2 vs. 31
32 vs. 33	31 vs. 34	16 vs. 17	15 vs. 18
16 vs. 49	15 vs. 50	8 vs. 25	7 vs. 26
17 vs. 48	18 vs. 47	9 vs. 24	10 vs. 23
8 vs. 57	7 vs. 58	4 vs. 29	3 vs. 30
25 vs. 40	26 vs. 39	13 vs. 20	14 vs. 19
9 vs. 56	10 vs. 55	5 vs. 28	6 vs. 27
24 vs. 41	23 vs. 42	12 vs. 21	11 vs. 22
4 vs. 61	3 vs. 62	16 Qualifiers	
29 vs. 36	30 vs. 35	1 vs. 16	2 vs. 15
13 vs. 52	14 vs. 51	8 vs. 9	7 vs. 10
20 vs. 45	19 vs. 46	4 vs. 13	3 vs. 14
5 vs. 60	6 vs. 59	5 vs. 12	6 vs. 11
28 vs. 37	27 vs. 38	8 Qualifiers	
12 vs. 53	11 vs. 54	1 vs. 8	2 vs. 7
21 vs. 44	22 vs. 43	4 vs. 5	3 vs. 6

Handicap Allowances

The USGA recommends the following handicap allowances in handicap competitions:

Singles match play: Allow the higher-handicapped player the full difference between the handicaps of the two players.

Four-ball match play: Reduce the handicaps of all four players by the handicap of the low-handicapped player, who shall then play from scratch. Allow each of the three other players 100 percent of the resulting difference.

Individual stroke play: Allow the full handicap.

Four-ball stroke play: Men — Allow each competitor 90 percent of his handicap. Women — Allow each competitor 95 percent of her handicap.

Best-ball-of-four, stroke play: Men — Allow each competitor 80 percent of his handicap. Women — Allow each competitor 90 percent of her handicap.

Optional Conditions

The following are some conditions which a Committee may wish to make:

The USGA periodically issues a List of Conforming Golf Balls. If it is desired to require use of a brand of golf ball on the List, the List should be posted and the following issued as a condition of the competition:

Only brands of golf balls on the USGA's latest List of Conforming Golf Balls may be used. Penalty for use of brand not on the List: Disqualification.

One-Ball Rule

If it is desired to prohibit changing brands of golf balls during a stipulated round, the following condition is recommended; it is suggested that it be considered only for competitions involving expert players:

Limitation on Golf Balls Used During Round
(Condition: Rules 5-1 and 33-1)

1. BALLS WITH IDENTICAL MARKINGS TO BE USED

Throughout a stipulated round, the player is limited to golf balls with identical markings, except that the player-identification numbers may differ by number only, not by color.

PENALTY FOR BREACH OF CONDITION:
Match play — At the conclusion of the hole at which the breach is discovered, the state of the match shall be adjusted by deducting one hole for each hole at which a breach occurred. Maximum deduction per round: two holes. Stroke play — Two strokes for each hole at which any breach occurred; maximum penalty per round: four strokes.

2. PROCEDURE WHEN BREACH DISCOVERED

When a player discovers that he has used a ball in breach of this condition, he shall abandon that ball before playing from the next teeing ground and complete the round using a proper ball; otherwise, *the player shall be disqualified.* If discovery is made during play of a hole and the player elects to substitute a proper ball before completing that hole, the player shall place a proper ball on the spot where the ball used in breach of this condition lay.

Time of Starting

If the Committee desires to adopt the condition in the Note under Rule 6-3a, the following wording is recommended:

Rule 6-3a provides: "The player shall start at the time laid down by the Committee." The penalty for breach of Rule 6-3a is disqualification. However, it is a condition of the competition that, if the player arrives at his starting point, ready to play, within five minutes after his starting time, in the absence of circumstances which warrant waiving the penalty of disqualification as provided in Rule 33-7, the penalty for failure to start on time is loss of the first hole in match play or two strokes at the first hole in stroke play instead of disqualification.

Practice

The Committee may make regulations governing practice in accordance with the Note to Rule 7-1, Clause (c) of the Exception under Rule 7-2 and Rule 33-2c.

Advice in Team Competitions

If the Committee desires to adopt the condition in the Note under Rule 8, which applies to a team competition with or without concurrent individual competition, the following wording is recommended:

In accordance with the Note to Rule 8 of the Rules of Golf, each team may appoint one person (in addition to the persons from whom advice may be asked under Rule 8-1) who may give advice (including pointing out a line for putting) to members of that team. Such person [if it is desired to put a restriction on who may be appointed, insert such restriction here] shall be identified to the Committee prior to the start of the competition.

Automotive Transportation

If it is desired to prohibit automotive transportation in a competition, the following condition is suggested:

Players shall not use automotive transportation during play.

PENALTY FOR BREACH OF CONDITION:
Match play — At the conclusion of the hole at which the breach is discovered, the state of the match shall be adjusted by deducting one hole for each hole at which a breach occurred. Maximum deduction per round: two holes.

Stroke play — Two strokes for each hole at which any breach occurred; maximum penalty per round: four strokes.

Match or stroke play — Use of any unauthorized automotive vehicle shall be discontinued immediately upon discovery that a breach has occurred. Otherwise, the player shall be disqualified.

Appendices II and III

Any design in a club or ball which is not covered by Rules 4 and 5 and Appendices II and III, or which might significantly change the nature of the game, will be ruled on by the United States Golf Association and the Royal and Ancient Golf Club of St. Andrews.

Note: Equipment approved for use or marketed prior to January 1, 1988 which conformed to the Rules in effect in 1987 but does not conform to the 1988 and subsequent Rules may be used until December 31, 1995; thereafter all equipment must conform to the current Rules.

Appendix II
DESIGN OF CLUBS

Rule 4-1 prescribes general regulations for the design of clubs. The following paragraphs, which provide some detailed specifications and clarify how Rule 4-1 is interpreted, should be read in conjunction with this Rule.

4-1a. General

ADJUSTABILITY — EXCEPTION FOR PUTTERS

Clubs other than putters shall not be designed to be adjustable except for weight.

Some other forms of adjustability are permitted in the design of a putter, provided that:

(i) the adjustment cannot be readily made;

(ii) all adjustable parts are firmly fixed and there is no reasonable likelihood of them working loose during a round; and

(iii) all configurations of adjustment conform with the Rules.

The disqualification penalty for purposely changing the playing characteristics of a club during a stipulated round (Rule 4-2) applies to all clubs, including a putter.

Note: It is recommended that all putters with adjustable parts be submitted to the United States Golf Association for a ruling.

4-1b. Shaft

GENERALLY STRAIGHT

The shaft shall be at least 18 inches (457mm) in length. It shall be straight from the top of the grip to a point not more than 5 inches (127mm) above the sole, measured along the axis of the shaft and the neck or socket.

BENDING AND TWISTING PROPERTIES

The shaft must be so designed and manufactured that at any point along its length:

(i) it bends in such a way that the deflection is the same regardless of how the shaft is rotated about its longitudinal axis; and

(ii) it twists the same amount in both directions.

ATTACHMENT TO CLUBHEAD

The neck or socket must not be more than 5 inches (127mm) in length, measured from the top of the neck or socket to the sole along its axis. The shaft and the neck or socket must remain in line with the heel, or with a point to the right or left of the heel, when the club is viewed in the address position. The distance between the axis of the shaft or the neck or socket and the back of the heel must not exceed 0.625 inches (16mm).

Exception for Putters: The shaft or neck or socket of a putter may be fixed at any point in the head and need not remain in line with the heel. The axis of the shaft from the top to a point not more than 5 inches (127mm) above the sole must diverge from the vertical in the toe-heel plane by at least 10 degrees when the club is in its normal address position.

4-1c. Grip

(i) For clubs other than putters the grip must be generally circular in cross-section, except that a continuous, straight, slightly raised rib may be incorporated along the full length of the grip.

(ii) A putter grip may have a non-circular cross-section, provided the cross-section has no concavity and remains generally similar throughout the length of the grip.

(iii) The grip may be tapered but must not have any bulge or waist.

(iv) For clubs other than putters the axis of the grip must coincide with the axis of the shaft.

(v) The cross-sectional dimension of a grip measured in any direction shall not exceed 1.75 inches (45mm).

(vi) A putter may have more than one grip, provided each is circular in cross-section and the axis of each coincides with the axis of the shaft.

Note: Putters approved for use or marketed prior to January 1, 1992 which are in breach of Clause (vi) may be used until December 31, 1992.

4-1d. Clubhead

DIMENSIONS

The dimensions of a clubhead (see diagram) are measured, with the clubhead in its normal address position, on horizontal lines between vertical projections of the outermost points of (i) the heel and the toe and (ii) the face and the back. If the outermost point of the heel is not clearly defined, it is deemed to be 0.625 inches (16mm) above the horizontal plane on which the club is resting in its normal address position.

PLAIN IN SHAPE

The clubhead shall be generally plain in shape. All parts shall be rigid, structural in nature and functional.

Features such as holes through the head, windows or transparencies, or appendages to the main body of the head such as plates, rods or fins for the purpose of meeting dimensional specifications, for aiming or for any other purpose are not permitted. Exceptions may be made for putters.

Any furrows in or runners on the sole shall not extend into the face.

4-1e. Club Face

GENERAL

Except for specified markings, the surface roughness must not exceed that of decorative sandblasting. Markings must not have sharp edges or raised lips, as determined by a finger test. The material and construction of the face shall not be designed or manufactured to have the effect at impact of a spring, or to impart significantly more spin to the ball than a standard steel face, or to have any other effect which would unduly influence the movement of the ball.

IMPACT AREA MARKINGS

Markings within the area where impact is intended (the "impact area") are governed by the following:

(i) *Grooves.* A series of straight grooves with diverging sides and a symmetrical cross-section may be used. (See diagram.) The width and cross-section must be generally consistent across the face of the club and along the length of the grooves. Any rounding of groove edges shall be in the form of a radius which does not exceed 0.020 inches (0.5mm). The width of the grooves shall not exceed 0.035 inches (0.9mm), using the 30 degree method of measurement on file with the United States Golf Association. The distance between edges of adjacent grooves must not be less than three times the width of a groove, and not less than 0.075 inches (1.9mm). The depth of a groove must not exceed 0.020 inches (0.5mm).

(ii) *Punch Marks.* Punch marks may be used. The area of any such mark must not exceed 0.0044 square inches (2.8 sq. mm). A mark must not be closer to an adjacent mark than 0.168 inches (4.3mm), measured from center to center. The depth of a punch mark must not exceed 0.040 inches (1.0mm). If punch marks are used in combination with grooves, a punch mark may not be closer to a groove than 0.168 inches (4.3mm), measured from center to center.

DECORATIVE MARKINGS

The center of the impact area may be indicated by a design within the boundary of a square whose sides are 0.375 inches (9.5mm) in length. Such a design must not unduly influence the movement of the ball. Decorative markings are permitted outside the impact area.

NON-METALLIC CLUB FACE MARKINGS

The above specifications do not apply to clubs on which the impact area of the face is non-metallic and whose loft angle is 24 degrees or less, but markings which could unduly influence the movement of the ball are prohibited. Clubs with this type of face and a loft angle exceeding 24 degrees may have grooves of maximum width 0.040 inches (1.0mm) and maximum depth 1½ times the groove width, but must otherwise conform to the markings specifications above.

PUTTER FACE MARKINGS

The specifications above with regard to club face markings do not apply to putters.

Appendix III
THE BALL

a. WEIGHT

The weight of the ball shall not be greater than 1.620 ounces avoirdupois (45.93gm).

b. SIZE

The diameter of the ball shall be not less than 1.680 inches (42.67mm). This specification will be satisfied if, under its own weight, a ball falls through a 1.680 inches diameter ring gauge in fewer than 25 out of 100 randomly selected positions, the test being carried out at a temperature of 23±1°C.

c. SPHERICAL SYMMETRY

The ball must not be designed, manufactured or intentionally modified to have flight properties which differ from those of a spherically symmetrical ball.

Furthermore the ball will not conform to the Rules of Golf if it fails to satisfy the performance specifications outlined below:

As described in procedures on file at the United States Golf Association, each ball type will be tested using 40 balls of that type, in 20 pairs. One ball of each pair will be launched spinning about one specified axis; the other ball of each pair will be launched spinning about a different, but also specified axis. Differences in carry and time of flight between the two balls of each pair will be recorded. If the mean of the differences in carry is greater than 3.0 yards, and that value is significant at the 5% level, OR if the mean of the differences in time of flight is greater than 0.20 seconds, and that value is significant at the 5% level, the ball type will not conform to the Rules of Golf.

Note: Methods of determining whether a ball performs as if it were generally spherically symmetrical may be subject to change as instrumentation becomes available to measure other properties accurately, such as aerodynamic coefficient of lift, coefficient of drag and moment of inertia.

d. INITIAL VELOCITY

The velocity of the ball shall not be greater than 250 feet (76.2m) per second when measured on apparatus approved by the United States Golf Association. A maximum tolerance of 2% will be allowed. The temperature of the ball when tested shall be 23±1°C.

e. OVERALL DISTANCE STANDARD

A brand of golf ball, when tested on apparatus approved by the USGA on the outdoor range at the USGA Headquarters under the conditions set forth in the Overall Distance Standard for golf balls on file with the USGA, shall not cover an average distance in carry and roll exceeding 280 yards plus a tolerance of 6%. *Note:* The 6% tolerance will be reduced to a minimum of 4% as test techniques are improved.

Appendix IV
MISCELLANEOUS
Par Computation

"Par" is the score that an expert golfer would be expected to make for a given hole. Par means errorless play without flukes and under ordinary weather conditions, allowing two strokes on the putting green.

Yardages for guidance in computing par are given below. They should not be applied arbitrarily; allowance should be made for the configuration of the ground, any difficult or unusual conditions and the severity of the hazards.

Each hole should be measured horizontally from the middle of the tee area to be used to the center of the green, following the line of play planned by the architect in laying out the hole. Thus, in a hole with a bend, the line at the elbow point should be centered in the fairway in accordance with the architect's intention.

YARDAGES FOR GUIDANCE

PAR	MEN	WOMEN
3	up to 250	up to 210
4	251 to 470	211 to 400
5	471 and over	401 to 575
6		576 and over

Flagstick Dimensions

The USGA recommends that the flagstick be at least seven feet in height and that its diameter be not greater than three-quarters of an inch from a point three inches above the ground to the bottom of the hole.

Protection of Persons Against Lightning

As there have been many deaths and injuries from lightning on golf courses, all clubs and sponsors of golf competitions are urged to take every precaution for the protection of persons against lightning.

Attention is called to Rules 6-8 and 33-2d.

The USGA suggests that players be informed that they have the right to stop play if they think lightning threatens them, even though the Committee may not have specifically authorized it by signal.

The USGA generally uses the following signals and recommends that all Committees do similarly:

Discontinue Play: Three consecutive notes of siren, repeated.

Resume Play: One prolonged note of siren, repeated.

Posters containing detailed information on protection from lightning are available from the USGA.

RULES OF AMATEUR STATUS

Any person who considers that any action he is proposing to take might endanger his amateur status should submit particulars to the United States Golf Association for consideration.

Definition of an Amateur Golfer

An amateur golfer is one who plays the game as a non-remunerative or non-profit-making sport.

Rule 1. Forfeiture of Amateur Status at Any Age

The following are examples of acts at any age which are contrary to the Definition of an Amateur Golfer and cause forfeiture of amateur status:

1. Professionalism

a. Receiving payment or compensation for serving as a professional golfer or identifying oneself as a professional golfer.

b. Taking any action for the purpose of becoming a professional golfer.

Note: Such actions include applying for a professional's position; filing application to a school or competition conducted to qualify persons to play as professionals in tournaments; receiving services from or entering into an agreement, written or oral, with a sponsor or professional agent; agreement to accept payment or compensation for allowing one's name or likeness as a skilled golfer to be used for any commercial purpose; and holding or retaining membership in any organization of professional golfers.

2. Playing for Prize Money

Playing for prize money or its equivalent in a match, tournament or exhibition.

Note: A player may participate in an event in which prize money or its equivalent is offered, provided that prior to participation he irrevocably waives his right to accept prize money in that event. (See USGA Policy on Gambling for definition of prize money.)

3. Instruction

Receiving payment or compensation for giving instruction in playing golf, either orally, in writing, by pictures or by other demonstrations, to either individuals or groups.

Exceptions:

1. Golf instruction may be given by an employee of an educational institution or system to students of the institution or system and by camp counselors to those in their charge, provided that the total time devoted to golf instruction during a year comprises less than 50 percent of the time spent during the year in the performance of all duties as such employee or counselor.

2. Payment or compensation may be accepted for instruction in writing, provided one's ability or reputation

as a golfer was not a major factor in one's employment or in the commission or sale of one's work.

4. Prizes, Testimonials and Gifts

a. Acceptance of a prize or testimonial of the following character (this applies to total prizes received for any event or series of events in any one tournament or exhibition, including hole-in-one or other events in which golf skill is a factor):

(i) Of retail value exceeding $500; or

(ii) Of a nature which is the equivalent of money or makes it readily convertible into money.

Exceptions:

1. Prizes of only symbolic value (such as metal trophies).

2. More than one testimonial award may be accepted from different donors even though their total retail value exceeds $500, provided they are not presented so as to evade the $500 value limit for a single award. (Testimonial awards relate to notable performances or contributions to golf, as distinguished from tournament prizes.)

b. Conversion of a prize into money.

c. Accepting expenses in any amount as a prize.

d. Because of golf skill or golf reputation, accepting in connection with any golfing event:

(i) Money, or

(ii) Anything else, other than merchandise of nominal value provided to all players.

5. Lending Name or Likeness

Because of golf skill or golf reputation, receiving or contracting to receive payment, compensation or personal benefit, directly or indirectly, for allowing one's name or likeness as a golfer to be used in any way for the advertisement or sale of anything, whether or not used in or appertaining to golf, except as a golf author or broadcaster as permitted by Rule 1-7.

6. Personal Appearance

Because of golf skill or golf reputation, receiving payment or compensation, directly or indirectly, for a personal appearance, except that reasonable expenses actually incurred may be received if no golf competition or exhibition is involved.

7. Broadcasting and Writing

Because of golf skill or golf reputation, receiving payment or compensation, directly or indirectly, for broadcasting concerning golf, a golf event or golf events, writing golf articles or books, or allowing one's name to be advertised or published as the author of golf articles or books of which one is not actually the author.

Exceptions:

1. Broadcasting or writing as part of one's primary occupation or career, provided instruction in playing golf is not included except as permitted in Rule 1-3.

2. Part-time broadcasting or writing, provided (a) the player is actually the author of the commentary, articles or books, (b) instruction in playing golf is not included except as permitted in Rule 1-3 and (c) the payment or compensation does not have the purpose or effect, directly or indirectly, of financing participation in a golf competition or golf competitions.

8. Golf Equipment

Because of golf skill or golf reputation, accepting golf balls, clubs, golf merchandise, golf clothing or golf shoes, directly or indirectly, from anyone manufacturing such merchandise without payment of current market price.

9. Membership and Privileges

Because of golf skill or golf reputation, accepting membership or privileges in a club or at a golf course without full payment for the class of membership or privileges involved unless such membership or privileges have been awarded (1) as purely and deservedly honorary,

(2) in recognition of an outstanding performance or contribution to golf and (3) without a time limit.

10. Expenses

Accepting expenses, in money or otherwise, from any source other than from a member of the player's family or legal guardian to engage in a golf competition or exhibition, or to improve golf skill.

Exceptions: A player may receive a reasonable amount of expenses as follows:

1. JUNIOR COMPETITIONS

As a player in a golf competition or exhibition limited exclusively to players who have not reached their 18th birthday.

2. INTERNATIONAL TEAMS

As a representative of a recognized golf association in an international team match between or among golf associations when such expenses are paid by one or more of the golf associations involved or, subject to the approval of the USGA, as a representative in an international team match conducted by some other athletic organization.

3. USGA PUBLIC LINKS CHAMPIONSHIPS

As a qualified contestant in the USGA Amateur Public Links Championships proper, but only within limits fixed by the USGA.

4. SCHOOL, COLLEGE, MILITARY TEAMS

As a representative of a recognized educational institution or of a military service in (1) team events or (2) other events which are limited to representatives of recognized educational institutions or of military serices, respectively. In each case, expenses may be accepted from only an educational or military authority.

5. INDUSTRIAL OR BUSINESS TEAMS

As a representative of an industrial or business golf team in industrial or business golf team competitions, respectively, but only within limits fixed by the USGA. (A statement of such limits may be obtained on request from the USGA.)

6. INVITATION UNRELATED TO GOLF SKILL

As a player invited for reasons unrelated to golf skill, e.g., a celebrity, a business associate or customer, a guest in a club-sponsored competition, etc., to take part in a golfing event.

Note 1: Except as otherwise provided in Exception 6 to Rule 1-10, acceptance of expenses from an employer, a partner or other vocational source is not permissible.

Note 2: Business Expenses — It is permissible to play in a golf competition while on a business trip with expenses paid provided that the golf part of the expenses is borne personally and is not charged to business. Further, the business involved must be actual and substantial, and not merely a subterfuge for legitimizing expenses when the primary purpose is golf competition.

Note 3: Private Transport — Acceptance of private transport furnished or arranged for by a tournament sponsor, directly or indirectly, as an inducement for a player to engage in a golf competition or exhibition shall be considered accepting expenses under Rule 1-10.

11. Scholarships

Because of golf skill or golf reputation, accepting the benefits of a scholarship or grant-in-aid other than in accord with the regulation of the National Collegiate Athletic Association, the Association of Intercollegiate

Athletics for Women, the National Association for Inter-collegiate Athletics, or the National Junior College Athletic Association.

12. Conduct Detrimental to Golf

Any conduct, including activities in connection with golf gambling, which is considered detrimental to the best interests of the game.

Rule 2. Advisory Opinions, Enforcement and Reinstatement

1. Advisory Opinions

Any person who considers that any action he is proposing to take might endanger his amateur status may submit particulars to the staff of the United States Golf Association for advice. If dissatisfied with the staff's advice, he may request that the matter be referred to the Amateur Status and Conduct Committee for decision. If dissatisfied with the Amateur Status and Conduct Committee's decision, he may, by written notice to the staff within 30 days after being notified of the decision, appeal to the Executive Committee, in which case he shall be given reasonable notice of the next meeting of the Executive Committee at which the matter may be heard and shall be entitled to present his case in person or in writing. The decision of the Executive Committee shall be final.

2. Enforcement

Whenever information of a possible act contrary to the Definition of an Amateur Golfer by a player claiming to be an amateur shall come to the attention of the United States Golf Association, the staff shall notify the player of the possible act contrary to the Definition of an Amateur Golfer, invite the player to submit such information as the player deems relevant and make such other investigation as seems appropriate under the circumstances. The staff shall submit to the Amateur Status and Conduct Committee all information provided by the player, their findings and their recommendation, and the Amateur Status and Conduct Committee shall decide whether an act contrary to the Definition of an Amateur Golfer has occurred. If dissatisfied with the Amateur Status and Conduct Committee's decision, the player may, by written notice to the staff within 30 days after being notified of the decision, appeal to the Executive Committee, in which case the player shall be given reasonable notice of the next meeting of the Executive Committee at which the matter may be heard and shall be entitled to present his case in person or in writing. The decision of the Executive Committee shall be final.

Upon a final decision of the Amateur Status and Conduct Committee or the Executive Committee that a player has acted contrary to the Definition of an Amateur Golfer, such Committee may require the player to refrain or desist from specified actions as a condition of retaining his amateur status or declare the amateur status of the player forfeited. Such Committee shall notify the player, if possible, and may notify any interested golf association of any action taken under this paragraph.

3. Reinstatement
a. AUTHORITY AND PRINCIPLES

Either the Executive Committee or its Amateur Status and Conduct Committee may reinstate a player to amateur status and prescribe the waiting period necessary for reinstatement or deny reinstatement. In addition, the Amateur Status and Conduct Committee may authorize the staff of the USGA to reinstate a player to amateur status and prescribe the waiting period necessary for reinstatement in situations where the acts contrary to the Definition of an Amateur Golfer are covered by ample precedent.

Each application for reinstatement shall be decided on its merits with consideration normally being given to the following principles:

(i) AWAITING REINSTATEMENT

The professional holds an advantage over the amateur by reason of having devoted himself to the game as his profession; other persons acting contrary to the Rules of Amateur Status also obtain advantages not available to the amateur. They do not necessarily lose such advantage merely by deciding to cease acting contrary to the Rules.

Therefore, an applicant for reinstatement to amateur status shall undergo a period awaiting reinstatement as prescribed.

The period awaiting reinstatement shall start from the date of the player's last act contrary to the Definition of an Amateur Golfer unless it is decided that it shall start from the date of the player's last known act contrary to the Definition of an Amateur Golfer.

(ii) PERIOD AWAITING REINSTATEMENT

A period awaiting reinstatement of two years normally will be required. However, that period may be *extended or shortened*. Longer periods normally will be required when applicants have played extensively for prize money or have been previously reinstated; shorter periods often will be permitted when applicants have acted contrary to the Rules for one year or less. A probationary period of one year normally will be required when an applicant's only act contrary to the Definition of an Amateur Golfer was to accept a prize of retail value exceeding $500.

(iii) PLAYERS OF NATIONAL PROMINENCE

Players of national prominence who have acted contrary to the Definition of an Amateur Golfer for more than five years normally will not be eligible for reinstatement.

(iv) STATUS DURING PERIOD AWAITING REINSTATEMENT

During the period awaiting reinstatement an applicant for reinstatement shall conform with the Definition of an Amateur Golfer.

He shall not be eligible to enter competitions limited to amateurs except that he may enter competitions solely among members of a club of which he is a member, subject to the approval of the club. He may also, without prejudicing his application, enter, as an applicant for reinstatement, competitions which are not limited to amateurs but shall not accept any prize reserved for an amateur.

b. FORM OF APPLICATION

Each application for reinstatement shall be prepared, in duplicate, on forms provided by the USGA.

The application must be filed through a recognized amateur golf association in whose district the applicant resides. The association's recommendation, if any, will be considered. If the applicant is unknown to the association, this should be noted and the application forwarded to the USGA, without prejudice.

c. OBJECTION BY APPLICANT

If dissatisfied with the decision with respect to his application for reinstatement, the applicant may, by written notice to the staff within 30 days after being notified of the decision, appeal to the Executive Committee, in which case he shall be given reasonable notice of the next meeting of the Executive Committee at which the matter may be heard and shall be entitled to present his case in person or in writing. The decision of the Executive Committee shall be final.

USGA Policy on Gambling

The Definition of an Amateur Golfer provides that an amateur golfer is one who plays the game as a non-remunerative or non-profit-making sport. When gambling motives are introduced, problems can arise which threaten the integrity of the game.

The USGA does not object to participation in wagering among individual golfers or teams of golfers when participation in the wagering is limited to the players, the players may only wager on themselves or their teams, the sole source of all money won by players is advanced by the players and the primary purpose is the playing of the game for enjoyment.

The distinction between playing for prize money and gambling is essential to the validity of the Rules of Amateur Status. Participation in wagering among individual golfers and participation in wagering among teams constitutes golf wagering and not playing for prize money.

On the other hand, organized amateur events open to the general golfing public and designed and promoted to create cash prizes are not approved by the USGA. Golfers participating in such events without irrevocably waiving their right to cash prizes are deemed by the USGA to be playing for prize money.

The USGA is opposed to and urges its Member Clubs, all golf associations and all other sponsors of golf competitions to prohibit types of gambling such as: (1) Calcuttas, (2) other auction pools, (3) pari-mutuels and (4) any other forms of gambling organized for general participation or permitting participants to bet on someone other than themselves or their teams.

The Association may deny amateur status, entry in USGA Championships and membership on USGA teams for international competitions to players whose activities in connection with golf gambling, whether organized or individual, are considered by the USGA to be contrary to the best interests of golf.

USGA Association Membership

USGA membership lets everyone know you've made an investment that brings great returns to all who play the game of golf.

As a USGA Member, you help the USGA keep golf the way you love it. As part of a nationwide network of dedicated golfers, you also receive special benefits, including a year of *Golf Journal*, a copy of *The Rules of Golf*, and more.

You can become a USGA Member for only $25, or you can choose a higher level with even more benefits. A USGA membership also makes a perfect gift.

Call today: 1-800-223-0041, or send in the coupon below.

Arnold Palmer
National Chairman

Yes, I want to invest at the following level:

☐ ADULT, $25   ☐ EAGLE CLUB, $100
☐ HUSBAND AND WIFE, $30   ☐ EAGLE CLUB Husband and Wife, $125
☐ JUNIOR (younger than 18), $15 ☐ GIFT

Name: _____
Spouse (if app.): _____
City: _____State: _____ Zip: _____

Friend's name to be enrolled at the level checked: _____
Friend's spouse's name (if app.): _____
City:_____State: _____Zip: _____
Enclosed is my check payable to USGA for $ _____ or
charge my

☐ Visa # _____   Exp: _____
☐ MasterCard # _____ Exp: _____
☐ American Express # _____   Exp: _____

Signed: _____

Mail this coupon to: USGA Members Program, P.O. Box 146, Golf House, Far Hills, NJ 07931-0746
or call 1-800-223-0041.